ALL OCCASION
COOKIES

Peanut Butter Knockouts, page 36

ALL OCCASION
COOKIES

RODALE

© 2004 by Rodale Inc.

Printed in the United States of America
Rodale Inc. makes every effort to use acid-free ∞, recycled paper ♻.

Cover photograph: Mitch Mandell
Cover recipe: Ultimate Chocolate Chip Oatmeal Cookies, courtesy of Swans Down Cake Flour, page 18; Double-Lemon Bars, courtesy of Land O'Lakes, page 59; Apricot & Cranberry White Chocolate Chunks, courtesy of Kraft Kitchens, page 102; Chocolate-dipped Refrigerator Cookies, courtesy of Domino Foods, page 114; Thumbprint Jewels, courtesy of Domino Foods, page 128; and Mom's Butter Cookies, courtesy of Land O'Lakes, page 120.
Food stylist: Diane Vezza
Illustrations: Judy Newhouse

Produced by:
BETH ALLEN ASSOCIATES, INC.

President/Owner: Beth Allen
Designer: Monica Elias
Art Production Director: Laura Smyth (smythtype)
Culinary Consultant/Food Editor: Deborah Mintcheff
Food Writer: Jean Galton
Copy Editor: Brenda Goldberg
Public Relations Consultants: Stephanie Avidon, Melissa Moritz
Nutritionist: Michele C. Fisher, Ph.D., R.D.

Library of Congress Cataloging-in-Publication Data

All occasion cookies.
   p. cm.
Includes index.
ISBN 1–57954–952–7 hardcover, tqc
ISBN 1–59486–060–9 hardcover, qtf
1. Cookies. I. Rodale (Firm)
TX772.A373 2004
641.5'854—dc22   2003022751

2 4 6 8 10 9 7 5 3 1   hardcover, tqc

2 4 6 8 10 9 7 5 3 1   hardcover, qtf

RODALE

WE **INSPIRE** AND **ENABLE** PEOPLE TO IMPROVE
THEIR LIVES AND THE WORLD AROUND THEM

FOR MORE OF OUR PRODUCTS

WWW.RODALESTORE.COM
(800) 848-4735

CONTENTS

INTRODUCTION

Oh-h-h-h sweet memories!

Remember some of the sweetest moments in your life and your family's? Chances are many are connected to cookies. Those days when you stood on your tiptoes to reach inside the cookie jar for one of Mom's Butter Cookies. Plus that holiday cookie-baking session you and your kids hold every year. And even those granola bars you bake and pack for your son in college. Now, those sweet memories can be made easier, and yes faster, than ever before. All it takes is this collection of 100 updated classic recipes inside *All Occasion Cookies*.

Flip though the pages to see scrumptious cookies, guaranteed to get you headed straight to your mixing bowl and cookie sheets. Naturally you'll find those old-fashioned favorites that are probably always in your cookie jar, such as Classic Chocolate Chips (page 82). And those beloved Chocolate Pinwheels (page 111), for which you can prepare the dough ahead and slice 'n' bake anytime in minutes. Browse through our "Best of the Bars" chapter and pick out one to stir up for dessert tonight. Choose the Raspberry & Cream Cheese Bars (page 48) and you'll have fancy dessert cookies that look and taste like they took hours to make. If you're in a hurry, make a batch of our *SuperQuick* peanut-buttery Zap-It Bars (page 51), guaranteed to get you in and out of the kitchen in fifteen minutes flat.

Kids will love this book too! They'll find Lollipop Cookies to put on sticks (page 67), and S'mores to stack in all flavors (page 74). If you crave lots of chocolate (who doesn't?), try the Chocolate Brownie Cookies (page 97), which get their deep, rich flavor from three different chocolates. But *All Occasion Cookies* is filled with more than "just sweetness and goodness." If you need some extra energy, check out our Fruity Carb Bars (page 42) and our Wholesome Granola Bars (page 45).

In our "Cookies on Holiday" chapter, you'll discover a year-long treasure trove of cookies to celebrate with. Look for Candy Cane Cookies (page 126) for hanging on the tree and a cookie pizza (page 134) for that Fourth of July picnic.

We've worked with the test kitchens of famous food companies across the country to bring you this collection of tried-and-true—as well as new—ideas for the cookie jar. All of the recipes need less than a half hour of hands-on fixing time, yet many are faster-fixing versions of old favorites. All come kitchen-tested to insure perfect results each time, even if you're just learning how to bake.

Just like the other books in our quick-cooking series, *All Occasion Cookies* brings you much more than a collection of fabulous recipes. Start with perusing our first chapter of "Cookies on the Fast Track." It's brimming with fresh ideas for speeding up your cookies, such as slicing and baking sugar cookies instead of making the time-consuming (but fun!) holiday cutouts that require a pastry board, a rolling pin, and cookie cutters.

This is just the start of our new quick-cooking world of cookies. Check out our Baking Basics feature on "Cookies Your Way" on page 11 to find out how to have cookies come out of the oven the way you like them—thin and crisp or thick and chewy. Then bake up a batch of the fastest cookies ever from "The Cookie Box" on page 12. Each one begins with a roll of refrigerated cookie dough and is *SuperQuick*, which means the cookies go from shopping bag to oven to cooling rack in less than thirty minutes.

Throughout the book, you'll also discover Cook to Cook tips which reveal baking secrets from other cooks just like you. Check out page 53 to find out the fastest way to get bar cookies out of the pan. And throughout the recipes, you'll find ways to speed up cookie baking with the microwave, such as melting chocolate or butter fast. Along the way, we've tucked in Food Facts for you to read and enjoy. Look on page 47 to find out what shortbread and petticoat tails have in common and on page 49 to find out how the brownie got its name.

Enjoy discovering all of the fabulous cookies, high-speed tips, and sound baking techniques we've tucked into *All Occasion Cookies*—realizing that you can look forward to even more great fast-cooking ideas in the other books in our collection. We've designed each cookbook with all the things you want in today's cookbooks—tips for saving time in the kitchen, information on cooking and baking basics, many great recipes that taste terrific, and of course plenty of beautiful photographs. Each book in our quick-cooking collection is designed to be not only enjoyable to browse through, but also chock full of information that you'll end up cherishing as a reliable kitchen helper and friend.

Have fun making, baking, and sharing our delicious *All Occasion Cookies*!

Pistachio White Chocolate Chip Cookies, page 101

Cookies on the Fast Track

Nothing's quite like the delicious aroma of cookies baking in the oven! Our quick-baking cookie collection is easy on the making and high on the taste. Get updated on the latest techniques, such as how to rotate your cookie sheets to get your favorite cookies in and out of the oven fast. Discover how to adjust a recipe to have cookies your way, just by adding a little extra sugar or buttering the pan. And how to turn a roll of refrigerated dough into many different tasty sweet treats. Or how to turn drop-cookie batter into bars when you're short on time. Get out your mixing bowl, head for the cupboard, stir up one of our recipes, and quick-bake a batch right now.

6 FAST WAYS TO SPEED UP YOUR COOKIES

DROP COOKIES The slow part of making drop cookies is baking batch after batch. Speed it up by using at least two cookie sheets and parchment paper. While the first batch of cookies bakes, drop the next batch onto sheets of parchment. After the first batch comes out, slide the parchment papers with unbaked cookies onto the sheets, then fast into the oven.

Professional bakers save time by using a small spring-loaded ice cream scoop to portion out the cookies. The scoop not only speeds up making the batches, but also all of the cookies will be much more uniform in size and shape.

Eliminate batches by converting your drop cookies into bar cookies. Most drop cookie doughs can be pressed into either a 9-inch square baking pan, a 13 × 9-inch rectangular or a 15 × 10-inch jellyroll pan for extra-thin cookies.

ROLLED COOKIES Making rolled, cut-out cookies takes lots of time. They're great for the holidays. Other times, speed up cookie shaping and baking by turning them into "slice and bakes." Shape the dough into logs about 1½ inches in diameter and wrap tightly. Refrigerate the dough for a few days or freeze for up to 3 months. When you're ready to bake, slice dough into ¼-inch-thick rounds and bake according to the recipe. Add about 3 to 5 minutes for baking frozen dough.

ON AND OFF THE PAN Cookie baking is quick, so quick that a few too many minutes in the oven result in dry, overcooked cookies. Prevent this by watching cookies carefully as they bake and by using the proper cookie sheets. *The Best*—Flat, heavy-gauge aluminum cookie sheets with a dull finish conduct heat well, bake cookies evenly, and turn them all golden-brown at the same time, provided the heat in the oven is evenly distributed. Double-thick insulated cookie sheets help prevent overbaking, though they can be expensive. *Avoid*—Dark nonstick or teflon-coated cookie sheets. These promote too much browning and can burn cookies.

Sweetie Pies, page 24

Mom's Butter Cookies, page 120

Caroling Cookies, page 122

LINE THEM! When baking cookies, line your pans with parchment paper or use flexible teflon baking sheets. These prevent cookies from sticking and make cleanup super easy. Teflon or silpat mats are the best choice, although they are an investment. Unlike parchment, they can be reused indefinitely.

ROLLING TIPS Make rolling out cookie dough easy as pie! When mixing the dough, reserve ¼ cup of the flour from the mixture. The dough will be slightly sticky. Pat the dough into flat rounds, not balls, then wrap tightly and chill. Use the reserved flour to dust the board or pastry cloth and rolling pin. This way, you keep the dough from sticking, but still are adding only the amount of flour called for in the recipe. Roll only a small amount of dough at a time, leaving the rest wrapped in the refrigerator. Roll from the middle out. Dip cutters in flour or confectioners' sugar to prevent them from sticking.

Baking Basics

COOKIES YOUR WAY—THIN & CRISP OR THICK & CHEWY!

Some people love thin and crisp cookies while others want them soft and chewy. Have cookies your way by following these tips:

THIN & CRISP

• Grease cookie sheets. This helps the cookies spread as they bake.

• Have all the ingredients at room temperature. If the butter in the dough is warm, it starts melting immediately when the cookies go into the oven, allowing the cookies to spread out thin.

• Add 1 to 2 tablespoons more of white sugar to the cookie dough. Since white sugar has less moisture than brown, it makes the cookies sandier and crisper in texture.

• Cool the cookies completely on wire racks. If cookies cool on a solid plate or cookie sheet, the moisture in the cookies gets trapped on the bottom of the cookies, turning crisp cookies soft and soggy. Racks let heat and moisture evaporate, leaving the cookies crisp and crunchy.

• Let the cookies cool completely before packing them away in airtight containers.

THICK & CHEWY

• Use cold ingredients, such as butter and eggs. As the colder dough hits the hot oven, it will not melt as quickly. This helps the cookies retain their shape.

• Use ungreased cookie sheets, which helps prevent spreading.

• If your cookie recipe uses both white and brown sugars, add 1 to 2 tablespoons more brown sugar. It contains more moisture than white sugar, so it makes softer cookies.

• Drop the cookies on cold cookie sheets. Before cooking the next batch, let the cookie sheets cool completely. Otherwise, the hot sheet will have time to melt and spread the cookies.

• Store the cookies in an airtight container with a piece of bread. This keeps moisture in the container and in the cookies.

KEEP THE SHAPE! To prevent cookies from spreading in the oven:
- **Chill the dough.** This will help cookies hold their shape, especially when baked in a hot oven. This technique is especially useful when making rolled out, shaped cookies. To achieve the best cookie shapes, chill the cookies after they are cut. Place them on a baking sheet in the refrigerator or freezer.
- **Substitute part shortening for some of the butter.** Since shortening does not melt as quickly in the oven as butter, it helps the cookie retain its shape.
- **Don't butter the cookie sheets.** Butter on the sheets helps the cookies spread. Use sheets of parchment or teflon baking sheets instead.

Baking Basics

THE COOKIE BOX

Start with a roll of refrigerated cookie dough. Crumble into a bowl and transform it into different cookies instantly. Bake as package directs.

THE FRUITIEST COOKIE Mix in ½ to ¾ cup of: dried cherries, cranberries, golden raisins, chopped prunes, apricots, peaches, pears.

THE NUTTIEST COOKIE Mix in ½ to ¾ cup of: one or more chopped, toasted hazelnuts, walnuts, pistachios, cashews, peanuts, almonds, pecans, or macadamias.

THE QUEEN OF CHIPS Mix in ½ to ¾ cup of chips: butterscotch, semisweet or bittersweet chocolate, milk chocolate, peanut butter, or white chocolate.

SPICE TWIRLS Stir in ¼ teaspoon cinnamon and ⅛ teaspoon nutmeg and cloves.

CANDYLAND CAKES Stir in ½ cup chopped candy bars, crushed peppermint sticks, or chopped peanut butter cups.

TROPICAL JOES Stir in ½ cup sweetened coconut, ½ cup chopped macadamias, and 1 teaspoon lime, lemon, or orange zest.

RUM RAISINS Stir in 1 teaspoon rum extract, ½ cup raisins, ¼ teaspoon orange zest. Consider using a mixture of dark and golden raisins in the dough.

PEANUT BUTTER Stir in ½ cup quick-cooking oats, ½ cup peanut butter chips, and ½ teaspoon cinnamon.

SANDWICHES When cookies are cooled, make them into ice cream sandwiches by filling them with vanilla or chocolate ice cream.

Roll the sides in chopped peanuts and refreeze until serving time.

CRUNCHY GRANOLA Stir in ½ cup granola. Bake as directed and while still warm, brush with melted apricot jelly.

JAM DOTS Shape dough into 1-inch balls and place 2 inches apart on ungreased cookie sheets. With your thumb, make an indentation in the center of each cookie. Dot with ½ teaspoon jam (blackberry, raspberry or apricot.) Bake for 10 to 13 minutes or until edges are light golden. Let cool before storing.

KISSES Break dough up and make 1-inch balls. Press an unwrapped chocolate kiss in the middle of each and set 2 inches apart on ungreased cookie sheets. Bake the cookies a little longer than package directs, until edges are light golden.

Chocolate-dipped Cranberry Cookies, page 98

THE BAKER'S SECRETS

Ask any good cookie baker about mixing up a cookie dough. You're likely to hear the suggestion: Bring all of the ingredients to room temperature before starting. The butter, sugar, and eggs need to be creamed together well, and this will not happen if the butter and eggs are cold. To hasten the chill-down, cut the butter into tiny pieces and spread them out in the bowl. For eggs, just immerse them a few minutes in warm water before cracking them open. It's fine to use an electric mixer on medium speed for the creaming part, but before adding the flour, reduce the speed to low. After adding the flour, never beat, a cookie dough, as it may toughen the cookies.

ROLLING OUT FASTER & FASTER

When you're making rolled cookies, mixing up the dough is fast and easy. But the rolling out, cutting out, and transferring cookies to the cookie sheets can "eat up" a lot of time. Here are a few tips to speed it all up: *First, chill the dough.* Pat it into a 5-inch disk, about 1-inch-thick, before putting it into the refrigerator. Chill the dough just until it's cold throughout, but not hard. If it's too cold, the dough will crack and crumble when you try to roll it out. If this happens, let the dough warm up to room temperature for a few minutes. Then knead it slightly in your hands to make it pliable again. *Use a pastry cloth,* plus a sleeve on the rolling pin, if you have them. (They'll help prevent sticking.) Rub flour into the cloth and sleeve before starting. *Before rerolling the scraps of dough,* pat them into a disk and rechill. *Not too thin, please!* Roll the dough ⅛-inch-thick, no thinner, as it might tear. Use a thin metal spatula to transfer cut-out cookies onto the cookie sheets.

SAVE TIME WITH THE BIG FREEZE

When making cookies, your freezer is one of your best kitchen helpers. If you have time, go ahead — make a double, or even a triple, batch. If you're making drop cookies, line a cookie sheet or pan (which will fit in your freezer) with parchment or waxed paper. Drop the cookies, placing them as close together as possible without allowing them to touch one another. Freeze until firm. Peel them off and place in a self-closing freezer bag. Use within three weeks. To bake, line the cookie sheets with parchment (preferably), or butter them generously. Preheat the oven as directed in the recipe. Place frozen cookies on prepared cookie sheets and put into the oven (do not defrost). Bake as directed in recipe, adding about 5 more minutes as needed.

For icebox / refrigerator cookies, shape the dough into logs of dough, 1½ inches in diameter. Wrap each log in plastic wrap or waxed paper and freeze. To bake, slice the frozen cookie dough into rounds ¼ inch thick. Bake as directed in the recipe, increasing the bake time about 5 minutes, or as needed. To freeze baked cookies, cool them completely on wire racks. do not ice, decorate, or roll in confectioners' sugar (though rolling in granulated sugar is fine). Pack in self-closing freezer bags. Stack bags flat into freezer. Use within one month. To defrost, transfer cookies to rack to defrost. After cookies have defrosted, follow the recipe directions for icing, decorating, or dusting with confectioners' sugar.

Raspberry & Cream Cheese Bars, page 48

Here are some of our favorite cookies to try:

Ultimate Chocolate Chip Oatmeal Cookies (page 18)

Raspberry & Cream Cheese Bars (page 48)

Double-Lemon Bars (page 59)

Our Very Best Brownies (page 60)

Peanut Blossoms (page 76)

Chocolate Toffee Bars (page 89)

Chocolate Pinwheels (page 111)

Melt-in-Your-Mouth Shortbread (page 112)

Browned-Butter Spritz (page 124)

Thumbprint Jewels (page 128)

Melt-in-Your-Mouth Shortbread, page 112

Chocolate Pinwheels, page 111

Fruit & Nut Cookies, page 32

In the Cookie Jar

Chances are your favorite cookies are the ones you keep in the cookie jar. The ever-loved chocolate chips, those peanut butter lunchbox favorites, and of course those must-have oatmeal raisins. You'll find a few others too—such as old-fashioned ginger melts, thimble cookies, and snickerdoodles. We've tucked in ways to mix up the dough quicker and some tricks for getting the cookies in and out of the oven faster. But we haven't stopped there. Look for fruit 'n' nut cookies, macaroons, and Chinese almond ones to keep your cookie jar filled up, too. You'll soon discover that it's fast, easy, and fun to keep your cookie jar bursting with tempting and tasty cookies—whatever the season.

ULTIMATE CHOCOLATE CHIP OATMEAL COOKIES

Prep **20 MINUTES**   *Bake* **10 MINUTES**

1¼	cups old-fashioned or quick oats
1	cup cake flour (not self-rising)
½	teaspoon baking powder
½	teaspoon baking soda
¼	teaspoon salt
½	cup unsalted butter, softened
½	cup granulated sugar
½	cup packed brown sugar
1	large egg
1	package (6 ounces) semisweet chocolate chips (1 cup)
2	ounces milk chocolate, coarsely grated

Double the chocolate and double the flavor in these cookies.

LET'S BEGIN Preheat the oven to 375°F. Lightly butter 2 cookie sheets. Process the oats in a food processor or blender to a fine powder. Add the flour, baking powder, baking soda, and salt and process for 30 seconds to mix.

CREAM & COMBINE Cream the butter and both of the sugars in a large bowl with an electric mixer on medium speed until light. Beat in the egg. Lower the speed and beat in flour mixture. Stir in chocolate chips and grated chocolate.

INTO THE OVEN Roll the dough into 1-inch balls and place 2 inches apart on the cookie sheets. Bake for 10 minutes, or until light brown. Transfer to wire racks to cool.

Makes 2 dozen

Per cookie: 150 calories, 2g protein, 21g carbohydrates, 7g fat, 4g saturated fat, 20mg cholesterol, 67mg sodium

---

Food Facts

5 DIFFERENT TYPES OF SUGARS USED IN COOKIE DOUGHS

Cookie recipes often call for different kinds of sugar. Here's how each contributes to flavor and texture. **Turbinado sugar**—The distinct, coarse crystals of this raw sugar result from a stream-cleaning process that leaves behind trace nutrients. It looks like maple-colored kosher salt. It tastes like white sugar with a slight molasses tang

Extra-fine or baker's sugar—This white sugar has more granules than regular sugar. So when it's creamed with butter, its extra granules trap in more air, giving cookies smoother tops and fewer cracks. **Bar sugar, superfine or ultrafine**— Look for these labels for the finest granulations of sugar; it's perfect for making coconut meringues.

Confectioners' powdered, or icing sugar—This sugar has been ground to a fine powder and then blended with cornstarch to prevent lumping. Sift before using in icing. **Brown sugar**—Surprisingly, brown sugar is simply granulated white sugar with some of the molasses added back in. "Light" and "dark" indicates how much molasses.

SOUR CREAM CHOCOLATE CHIP COOKIES

Prep **20 MINUTES**   *Bake* **10 MINUTES**

2	cups all-purpose flour
½	teaspoon baking powder
½	teaspoon baking soda
½	teaspoon salt
⅔	cup butter softened
½	cup granulated sugar
½	cup packed brown sugar
½	cup sour cream
1	large egg
1	teaspoon vanilla extract
1	package (6 ounces) semisweet chocolate chips (1 cup)
1	cup chopped pecans or walnuts (optional)

The addition of sour cream makes (and keeps!) these cookies delectably moist. Space the cookies a good 2 inches apart on the cookie sheet so they have plenty of room to spread out.

LET'S BEGIN Preheat the oven to 350°F. Grease 2 large cookie sheets. For the flour mixture, combine the first four ingredients in a medium bowl.

CREAM & COMBINE Cream the butter and both of the sugars in a large bowl with an electric mixer on medium speed until light and fluffy. Blend in the sour cream, egg, and vanilla. Reduce the speed to low and blend in the flour mixture. Stir in the chocolate chips and nuts, if using.

OFF THE SPOON Drop heaping teaspoonfuls of the dough on the sheets. Bake for 10 to 12 minutes, or until golden brown. Transfer the cookies to wire racks to cool.

Makes 3½ dozen cookies
Per cookie: 94 calories, 1g protein, 12g carbohydrates, 5g fat, 3g saturated fat, 14mg cholesterol, 83mg sodium

---

Time Savers

THE QUICK SCOOP ON DROP COOKIES

Here's a speedy way to get cookie dough onto cookie sheets in record time: scoop, don't drop, the dough. It not only speeds up dropping the cookie dough onto the sheets but also makes the cookies a uniform size. This means all of the cookies will be done at the same time.

All you need is an ice cream scoop, preferably one with a spring-loaded mechanism that pushes out the dough fast. If you have one in your kitchen drawer, chances are it's a bit larger than the one you need here. Cookware stores carry scoops in several sizes: 1¼-inch one for small cookies, 2 inches for oversized cookies.

Scooping goes the fastest with chilled cookie dough because it doesn't stick to the scoop as much as a soft warm dough. Spray the scoop with nonstick spray to help it release the dough even easier. An added benefit: cookies made with a chilled dough keep their shapes better in the oven than a soft dough. They don't spread and flatten out as much during baking and make softer cookies.

STIX 'N' STONES

Prep **25 MINUTES**   *Microwave* **2 MINUTES**

1	cup white chocolate chips
1	cup peanut butter chips
1	cup milk chocolate and hazelnut spread
1	cup hazelnuts, toasted and chopped (see opposite page)
1	cup salted cocktail peanuts
2	cups chow mein noodles
½	cup dried cranberries

If you have never tasted that wonderfully decadent chocolate-hazelnut spread that's in your grocer's these days, you're in for a delicious treat. For breakfast, spread it on toast—hmmm good.

LET'S BEGIN Line 2 cookie sheets with foil. Put the white chocolate and the peanut butter chips in a microwavable bowl. Microwave on Medium for 2 minutes and stir until smooth. (Or melt chips in the top of a double boiler.)

MELT & MIX Stir in the hazelnut spread until smooth. Gently fold in the peanuts, noodles, and cranberries.

OFF THE SPOON Drop the mixture by heaping table-spoonfuls on the sheets. Cool until set. Store between layers of wax paper in an airtight container.

Makes 3 dozen cookies

Per cookie: 160 calories, 4g protein, 17g carbohydrates, 10g fat, 4g saturated fat, 0mg cholesterol, 68mg sodium

THIMBLE COOKIES

Prep **30 MINUTES**   *Chill* **1 HOUR**   *Bake* **16 MINUTES**

1   cup butter or margarine, softened

½   cup superfine sugar, plus additional for rolling (optional)

¼   teaspoon salt

2   large egg yolks

1   teaspoon vanilla extract

3   cups all-purpose flour

Assorted jams, jellies, or frosting for filling

Here's a variation on those traditional thumbprint cookies. Instead of using your thumb to quickly make an indentation in each, use a thimble. Before serving, fill each with a colorful jam.

LET'S BEGIN Cream the butter, sugar, and salt in a large bowl with an electric mixer on medium speed until light and fluffy. Add the egg yolks and vanilla and beat until light. Reduce the speed to low and gradually beat in the flour until blended. Chill for 1 hour.

INTO THE OVEN Preheat the oven to 375°F. Shape the dough into ¾-inch balls and roll each in sugar, if you like. Place 1 inch apart on ungreased cookie sheets. Make a "cup" in the center of each ball with a thimble. Place on unbaked cookie sheets. Bake for 16 to 18 minutes, until light brown. Cool completely. Before serving, fill centers with jam, jelly, or frosting.

Makes about 6½ dozen cookies

Per cookie: 77 calories, 1g protein, 7g carbohydrates, 5g fat, 3g saturated fat, 14mg cholesterol, 2mg sodium

Baking Basics

TOASTING HAZELNUTS YOUR WAY

OVEN METHOD

Preheat the oven to 325°F. Spread out the nuts in a baking pan. Bake for 10 minutes, or until the nuts are golden and the skins begin to flake off, shaking the pan. Wrap the nuts in a clean kitchen towel and rub the nuts together to remove the skins.

SKILLET METHOD

Put the hazelnuts in a large dry skillet and toast over medium heat for 8 minutes, or until nuts are golden and the skins begin to flake off. Shake the skillet several times. Wrap the nuts in a clean kitchen towel and rub the nuts together to remove the skins.

SWEETIE PIES

Prep **30 MINUTES**   *Bake* **20 MINUTES**

1   can (21 ounces) cherry
      filling and topping

1   teaspoon almond extract

½   cup butter or margarine,
      softened

1   package (3 ounces)
      cream cheese, softened

1   tablespoon granulated
      sugar

1⅓ cups all-purpose flour

½   cup finely chopped
      pecans

These tiny two-bite pies look like a cookie but taste like a pie. They're as perfect at a fancy tea party as an after-school snack.

LET'S BEGIN Preheat oven to 350°F. Set out a miniature muffin pan (with 1¾ × 1-inch cups). Mix the cherry filling and the almond and set aside. Cream the butter, cream cheese, and sugar in a large bowl with an electric mixer on medium speed until light and fluffy. Stir in the flour and the pecans.

SHAPE & FILL Roll dough into 1-inch balls. Press each ball into the bottom and up the sides of in a miniature muffin pan cup. Fill each with about 1 teaspoon cherry filling.

INTO THE OVEN Bake cookies for 20 to 25 minutes, or just until lightly brown. Cool in pans for 5 minutes, then transfer to wire rack and cool completely.

Makes 2 dozen
Per cookie: 120 calories, 1g protein, 13g carbohydrates, 7g fat, 3g saturated fat, 15mg cholesterol, 56mg sodium

LEMON BUTTER PECAN COOKIES

Prep **20 MINUTES**   *Microwave* **2 MINUTES**   *Bake* **9 MINUTES**

1   package (10 ounces)
      white chips (1⅔ cups)

2¼   cups all-purpose flour

¾   cup sugar

2   large eggs

¾   teaspoon baking soda

½   teaspoon freshly grated
      lemon zest

¼   teaspoon lemon extract

½   cup butter or margarine

¾   cup chopped pecans

Lemon Drizzle (see recipe)

The rich taste of a homemade butter cookie can't be beat. And this one has the added surprise of white chocolate chips and fresh lemon zest. These make delicious cookies to serve with ice cream or sorbet.

LET'S BEGIN Preheat oven to 350°F. Reserve 2 tablespoons of the chips for the drizzle. Combine flour, sugar, eggs, baking soda, lemon zest, and lemon extract in large bowl.

MICROWAVE & MIX Put the remaining chips and butter in a microwavable bowl. Microwave on High for 1 minute and stir. If necessary, cook and stir in 15-second intervals, just until chips are melted. Blend into flour mixture. Stir in pecans. Drop by rounded teaspoons onto ungreased cookie sheets.

INTO THE OVEN Bake cookies for 9 to 11 minutes, or just until very slightly golden around edges (do not overbake). Transfer to a wire rack and cool completely. Decorate cookies with Lemon Drizzle.

LEMON DRIZZLE

Put 2 tablespoons white chips and ½ teaspoon shortening (do not use butter, margarine, spread or oil) in a small microwavable bowl. Cook on High for 1 minute and stir until smooth. Stir in a few drops of yellow food color and a few drops lemon extract, if you wish.

> **Makes about 3½ dozen cookies**
> *Per cookie: 110 calories, 1g protein, 13g carbohydrates, 6g fat, 3g saturated fat, 16mg cholesterol, 60mg sodium*

Black Forest Cookies

Prep **30 MINUTES**   *Bake* **12 MINUTES**

¾   **cup all-purpose flour**

¼   **teaspoon baking powder**

1   **package (11½ ounces) milk chocolate chips (2 cups)**

¼   **cup butter, softened**

½   **cup packed brown sugar**

2   **large eggs**

1   **teaspoon vanilla extract**

1   **package (6 ounces) cherry-flavored dried cranberries**

1   **cup pecans or walnuts, coarsely chopped**

These cookies are a fast twist on black forest cake, which contains chocolate, cherries, and cherry brandy. They're named for the best brandy that comes from Swabia in Germany's Black Forest region.

LET'S BEGIN Preheat the oven to 350°F. Grease a cookie sheet. Combine the flour and baking powder in a bowl. Put ¾ cup of the chips in a large microwavable bowl. Cook on High for 2 minutes. Stir until the chocolate melts.

MIX IT IN Stir the butter into the melted chocolate until melted. Stir in the brown sugar, eggs, and vanilla. Add the flour mixture, mixing until thoroughly combined. Stir in the remaining chocolate chips, the dried cranberries, and nuts.

INTO THE OVEN Drop tablespoonfuls of the dough onto cookie sheets. Bake for 12 minutes, or until the cookies puff and are set. For firmer cookies, bake for 14 minutes. Cool for 2 minutes. Transfer to wire racks to cool completely.

Makes about 2½ dozen cookies

Per cookie: 140 calories, 1g protein, 17g carbohydrates, 7g fat, 3g saturated fat, 20mg cholesterol, 25mg sodium

CLASSIC OATMEAL-RAISIN COOKIES

Prep **30 MINUTES**   Bake **12 MINUTES**

1	cup all-purpose flour
1	teaspoon ground cinnamon
½	teaspoon baking soda
¼	teaspoon salt
¾	cup unsalted butter, softened
1	cup packed brown sugar
½	cup granulated sugar
¼	cup milk
1	large egg
1	teaspoon vanilla extract
3	cups old-fashioned oats
1	cup coarsely chopped walnuts (optional)
1	cup dark raisins

Here are the old-fashioned oatmeal-raisin cookies from childhood days. For a change, substitute for the dark raisins: dried cherries, dried cranberries, chopped dried apricots, or golden raisins.

LET'S BEGIN Preheat the oven to 350°F. Mix flour, cinnamon, baking soda, and salt in a bowl.

CREAM & COMBINE Cream the butter, both of the sugars, the milk, egg, and vanilla in a large bowl with an electric mixer on medium-high speed until light and fluffy. Stir in the flour mixture with a wooden spoon, then stir in the remaining ingredients until well mixed.

INTO THE OVEN Drop heaping teaspoonfuls of the dough onto ungreased cookie sheets. Bake for 12 minutes, or until the cookies are golden and crisp (do not overbake). Transfer to wire racks to cool completely.

Makes 3 dozen cookies
Per cookie: 122 calories, 2g protein, 19g carbohydrates, 5g fat, 3g saturated fat, 17mg cholesterol, 40mg sodium

---

Food Facts

THE 4 MOST COMMON FORMS OF OATS

When buying oats for making cookies, read the labels! There are several oats on the market—some are cookie-friendly, others are not. All have been cleaned, toasted, hulled, and cleaned again. From this point on, differences in processing and packaging yield vastly different products.

Old-fashioned rolled oats are rolled until flattened. Go for these when you want a bit more chew and texture in your cookies.

Quick-cooking rolled oats are first cut into pieces, then steamed and rolled into thinner flakes (they cook up faster). These two can be interchangeable in cookie recipes.

Instant oats are rolled thinner and cut into even smaller pieces with flavorings added. Not good for baking since they loose their form.

Scotch oats (also called steel-cut oats and Irish oatmeal) have been cut into 2 or 3 pieces, but not rolled. They take longer to cook. and are not good for baking.

Pineapple-Oatmeal "Scotchies"

PINEAPPLE-OATMEAL "SCOTCHIES"

Prep **30 MINUTES**   *Bake* **20 MINUTES**

3	cups old-fashioned oats
2	cups all-purpose flour
1	teaspoon baking powder
1	teaspoon ground cinnamon
½	teaspoon salt
1½	cups butter or margarine, softened
1½	cups packed brown sugar
2	cans (8 ounces each) crushed pineapple, drained
1	large egg
1	package (6 ounces) butterscotch chips (1 cup)

The molasses in the brown sugar and the butterscotch chips team up here to deliver great old-fashioned flavor to these cookies.

LET'S BEGIN Preheat the oven to 375°F. Spray 2 cookie sheets with nonstick cooking spray. Combine the oats, flour, baking powder, cinnamon, and salt in a large bowl.

CREAM & COMBINE Beat the butter and sugar in another large bowl with an electric mixer on medium speed until light. Beat in the pineapple and egg. Reduce speed to low and blend in oat mixture. Stir in the chips.

INTO THE OVEN Drop rounded tablespoonfuls on the sheets. Flatten each gently with a spoon. Bake for 20 minutes, or until golden. Transfer to wire racks to cool completely.

Makes 3½ dozen cookies

Per cookie: 157 calories, 2g protein, 21g carbohydrates, 7g fat, 2g saturated fat, 7mg cholesterol, 120mg sodium

SuperQuick
EASY COCONUT MACAROONS

Prep **10 MINUTES**   *Bake* **10 MINUTES**

1	can (14 ounces) sweetened condensed milk
2	packages (7 ounces each) flaked sweetened coconut
1½	teaspoons imitation almond extract

Make these macaroons larger if you wish. Just add a little baking time.

LET'S BEGIN Preheat the oven to 350°F. Grease 2 cookie sheets. Blend all the ingredients together in a large bowl. Drop teaspoonfuls of the mixture on the cookie sheets.

INTO THE OVEN Bake for 10 to 12 minutes. Transfer the macaroons to wire racks to cool completely.

Makes 22 cookies

Per cookie: 131 calories, 2g protein, 16g carbohydrates, 7g fat, 6g saturated fat, 6mg cholesterol, 71mg sodium

B-I-G Fruit & Oatmeal Cookies

Prep **25 minutes**   *Bake* **17 minutes**

1½	cups all-purpose flour
1	teaspoon baking soda
½	teaspoon ground cinnamon
½	teaspoon ground nutmeg
1	medium orange
¾	cup butter or margarine, softened
1¼	cups sugar
1	large egg
1	medium apple, not peeled, cored and chopped (about 1 cup)
2	cups quick-cooking oats
½	cup walnuts or pecans, chopped

Sugar and spice and everything nice—in this case orange, apple, and nuts—and naturally great flavor and texture, too. Baking up a quarter cup of dough for each cookie makes them big and bold.

LET'S BEGIN Preheat the oven to 375°F. Lightly grease 2 large cookie sheets. For the flour mixture, whisk the first four ingredients together in a large bowl. Grate the orange peel. Dice the orange pulp and place in a strainer to drain.

STIR IT TOGETHER Combine the butter and sugar in a large bowl, beating well with a wooden spoon until blended. Beat in the egg and orange zest. Gradually stir in the flour mixture, then stir in the diced orange, apple, oats, and nuts.

INTO THE OVEN Drop one-quarter cupfuls of the dough on the cookie sheets (6 to 9 cookies will fit at one time). Gently pat the dough to form 3-inch rounds. Bake for 17 to 20 minutes, until the edges just begin to brown. Cool for 1 or 2 minutes, then transfer the cookies to wire racks to cool completely. For soft cookies, store in an airtight container. Or, store loosely covered for crisp cookies.

Makes 1 dozen cookies

Per cookie: 196 calories, 3g protein, 26g carbohydrates, 10g fat, 5g saturated fat, 29mg cholesterol, 134mg sodium

CHEDDAR-APPLE KICKOFF COOKIES

Prep **20 MINUTES**   *Bake* **10 MINUTES**

1¼   cups all-purpose flour

1   teaspoon baking soda

¼   teaspoon salt

½   teaspoon ground nutmeg

½   cup unsalted butter, softened

1   cup packed brown sugar

½   cup shredded Cheddar cheese

2   large eggs

1   teaspoon vanilla extract

3   cups old-fashioned oats

⅔   cup applesauce

Lots of old-fashioned rolled oats, tasty applesauce, shredded Cheddar, and just the right amount of spice makes these fast cookies perfect for snacking during football season. Touchdown!

LET'S BEGIN Preheat oven to 350°F. Butter 2 cookie sheets. Mix flour, baking soda, salt, and nutmeg in a bowl.

CREAM & COMBINE Cream butter, brown sugar, and Cheddar in a large bowl with an electric mixer on medium speed until light. Beat in eggs and vanilla. Reduce speed to low and blend in flour mixture. Stir in oats and applesauce.

INTO THE OVEN Drop teaspoonfuls of the dough on the cookie sheets. Bake for 10 to 12 minutes, until golden. Transfer the cookies to wire racks to cool completely.

Makes 3 dozen cookies

Per cookie: 102 calories, 2g protein, 15g carbohydrates, 4g fat, 2g saturated fat, 21mg cholesterol, 68mg sodium

FRUIT & NUT COOKIES

Prep **20 MINUTES**   *Bake* **10 MINUTES**

½   cup packed brown sugar

¼   cup oil

2   tablespoons water

2   large egg whites, slightly beaten

1   teaspoon ground cinnamon

½   teaspoon baking soda

⅛   teaspoon salt

1½   cups raisin bran cereal

1   cup all-purpose flour

¼   cup chopped walnuts

¼   cup chopped dried apricots, dried cherries, or cranberries (optional)

Here's a healthy bran cookie with fruits and nuts that spans the seasons. Add dried apricots to the batter in the spring, dried cherries in the fall, and cranberries at holiday time.

LET'S BEGIN Preheat the oven to 350°F. Spray 2 cookie sheets with nonstick cooking stray. Stir the first seven ingredients together in a large bowl until well blended.

MIX & DROP Add the bran and flour and stir just until the flour disappears. Mix in the walnuts and apricots, if you wish. Drop by rounded teaspoonfuls, 2 inches apart, onto cookie sheets.

INTO THE OVEN Bake for 10 minutes, or until cookies are lightly brown around the edges. Transfer the cookies to wire racks to cool completely.

Makes 3½ dozen
Per cookie: 44 calories, 1g protein, 7 g carbohydrates, 2g fat, 0g saturated fat, 0mg cholesterol, 29mg sodium

DROP SUGAR COOKIES

Prep **25 MINUTES** *Bake* **8 MINUTES**

2	cups cake flour (not self-rising), sifted
1¼	teaspoons baking powder
½	teaspoon salt
⅔	cup butter
¾	cup sugar, plus additional for sprinkling (optional)
1	large egg
¼	teaspoon lemon extract
1	teaspoon vanilla extract
⅓	cup milk

Sprinkling cookies with sugar before baking adds a bit more sparkle and sweetness. Use granulated, turbinado, or colored sugar.

LET'S BEGIN Preheat the oven to 375°F. Whisk the flour, baking powder, and salt together in a large bowl.

CREAM & COMBINE Beat the butter in a large bowl with an electric mixer on medium speed until creamy. Gradually add the sugar, beating until light and fluffy. Beat in the egg, lemon extract, and vanilla. Reduce the speed to low and add the flour mixture alternately with the milk.

INTO THE OVEN Drop teaspoonfuls of the batter on ungreased baking sheets. Sprinkle with sugar, if you like. Bake for 8 to 10 minutes. Transfer to wire racks to cool completely.

Makes 4 dozen cookies

Per cookie: 55 calories, 1g protein, 7g carbohydrates, 3g fat, 2g saturated fat, 12mg cholesterol, 65mg sodium

Cook to Cook

WHAT'S THE BEST COOKIE JAR?

❝My favorite cookie jar is a *tall clear plastic canister* with a metal clip that seals tightly and keep cookies fresh for days. You can quickly see at a glance what kind of cookies are in the jar, plus how many are left.

Metal cookie cans are great too as they seal out the moisture in the air and keep crisp cookies crisp and soft cookies soft.

My most treasured cookie jar is *an old-fashioned, hand-painted ceramic one* in the shape of a baker that my grand-mother gave me (his baker's hat is the lid). Quite a conversation piece, but the lid doesn't fit tightly, so theoretically the cookies lose their freshness faster. However, cookies in our house never last long enough to go stale, so I can't really be sure!❞

SNICKERDOODLES

Prep **45 MINUTES**   *Bake* **8 MINUTES**

COOKIES

2¾	cups all-purpose flour
2	teaspoons cream of tartar
1	teaspoon baking soda
¼	teaspoon salt
1	cup butter, softened
1½	cups sugar
2	large eggs
1	teaspoon vanilla extract

CINNAMON-SUGAR COATING

3	tablespoons sugar
1½	teaspoons ground cinnamon

Take a trip back to eighteenth-century England, which is how long these cookies have been enjoyed. They always contains spices and sometimes dried fruit and nuts and are usually rolled in sugar.

LET'S BEGIN Preheat the oven to 400°F. Mix the flour, cream of tartar, baking soda, and salt together. Cream the butter and sugar with an electric mixer on medium speed. Beat in eggs and vanilla. Stir in the flour mixture.

STIR & SHAPE Mix the sugar and cinnamon. Shape dough into 1-inch balls then roll in the sugar until coated.

INTO THE OVEN Place 2 inches apart on ungreased cookie sheets. Bake for 8 to 10 minutes, until the edges are light brown. Transfer the cookies to wire racks to cool.

Makes 4 dozen cookies
Per cookie: 92 calories, 1g protein, 12g carbohydrates, 4g fat, 3g saturated fat, 20mg cholesterol, 823mg sodium

GINGER MELTS

Prep **30 MINUTES**   *Chill* **30 MINUTES**   *Bake* **11 MINUTES**

2½ cups all-purpose flour

2 teaspoons ground cinnamon

1 teaspoon ground ginger

½ teaspoon baking soda

¼ teaspoon salt

1 cup unsalted butter or margarine, softened

1⅓ cups packed dark brown sugar

¼ cup light (mild) molasses

1 large egg

⅓ cup granulated sugar + extra for sprinkling

Butter gives these cookie-jar favorites great flavor and the molasses keeps them moist. Dark brown sugar gives them the richest flavor, but you can use light brown sugar, if you like.

LET'S BEGIN Preheat the oven to 375°F. Grease 2 cookie sheets. For the flour mixture, combine the first five ingredients in a large bowl.

CREAM & COMBINE Cream the butter and brown sugar in a large bowl with an electric mixer on medium speed until light and fluffy. Add the molasses and beat until well mixed. Add the egg and beat until mixed well. Reduce the speed to low and gradually blend in the flour mixture. Cover the dough and refrigerate for 30 minutes, or until firm.

INTO THE OVEN Roll the dough into 1-inch balls. Roll in the granulated sugar and place on the cookie sheets. Bake for 11 to 14 minutes, until light brown around the edges. Sprinkle the cookies with additional sugar, if you like. Transfer to wire racks to cool completely.

Makes about 3 dozen cookies

Per cookie: 125 calories, 1g protein, 18g carbohydrates, 6g fat, 3g saturated fat, 20mg cholesterol, 41mg sodium

PEANUT BUTTER KNOCKOUTS

Prep **30 MINUTES**   *Bake* **8 MINUTES**   *Microwave* **1 MINUTE**

1   package (17½ ounces)
     home-style peanut
     butter cookie mix

1   package (3 ounces)
     cream cheese, softened

3   tablespoons smooth
     peanut butter

1   large egg yolk

1½   tablespoons sugar

Dash of salt (optional)

⅓   cup mini semisweet
     chocolate chips
     (optional)

⅓   cup semisweet chocolate
     chips

2   tablespoons vegetable
     shortening

Peanut butter and chocolate are a match made in heaven. Melting chocolate with a bit of vegetable shortening guarantees that the chocolate will remain nice and shiny.

LET'S BEGIN Preheat the oven to 375°F. Prepare the cookie mix according to package directions. Roll the dough into 36 balls (1 inch in diameter). Place the balls about 2 inches apart on ungreased cookie sheets. Make an indentation in the center of each cookie with your thumb.

CREAM & COMBINE Beat the cream cheese, peanut butter, egg yolk, sugar, and salt, if using, in a medium bowl with an electric mixer on medium speed until blended. Stir in the mini chocolate chips, if you like.

INTO THE OVEN Fill the center of each cookie with a rounded teaspoon of the cream-cheese mixture. Bake for 8 to 10 minutes, until golden brown. Cool the cookies for 2 minutes, then transfer to wire racks to cool completely. Combine the semisweet chocolate chips and shortening in a microwavable bowl. Microwave on High for 30 seconds, then stir. Continue to cook in 15 second intervals, if necessary, until melted. Drizzle the chocolate over the cookies with a fork. Allow the chocolate to set before storing.

Makes 3 dozen cookies
Per cookie: 173 calories, 3g protein, 18g carbohydrates,
11g fat, 3g saturated fat, 19mg cholesterol, 134mg sodium

OKEECHOBEE BOBBERS

Prep **45 MINUTES**   *Bake* **8 MINUTES**

The shape of these round little orange-buttery cookies is reminiscent of the round shape of the floating bobbers used while fishing.

1	cup butter, softened
2	cups sugar
3	large eggs
1	teaspoon baking powder
1	teaspoon salt
1	teaspoon orange extract
1	teaspoon vanilla extract
3½	cups all-purpose flour
½	cup flaked sweetened coconut

LET'S BEGIN Preheat the oven to 350°F. Butter two cookie sheets. Beat the first seven ingredients together in a bowl with an electric mixer on low speed for 2 to 3 minutes.

BLEND IT IN Stir in the flour and coconut by hand and beat for 2 to 3 minutes, until well mixed.

INTO THE OVEN Drop the dough, 2 inches apart, by rounded teaspoonfuls on cookie sheets. Bake for 8 to 12 minutes, until edges are light brown. Transfer the cookies to wire racks to cool completely.

Makes 5 dozen cookies
Per cookie: 90 calories, 1g protein, 13g carbohydrates, 4g fat, 2g saturated fat, 20mg cholesterol, 80mg sodium

CHINESE ALMOND COOKIES

Prep **35 MINUTES**   *Bake* **11 MINUTES**

These ever-popular Chinese bake-shop cookies are doubly good, due to the almond extract and whole blanched almonds. Serve them the next time you have Chinese take-out.

2¼	**cups all-purpose flour**
1	**teaspoon baking powder**
¼	**teaspoon salt**
1	**cup butter, softened**
¾	**cup sugar**
1	**large egg**
1	**teaspoon almond extract**
48	**whole blanched almonds**
1	**large egg yolk**
1	**tablespoon water**

LET'S BEGIN Preheat the oven to 350°F. For the flour mixture, whisk the first three ingredients in a medium bowl.

CREAM & COMBINE Cream the butter and sugar in a large bowl with an electric mixer on medium speed until light and fluffy. Add the egg and almond extract and beat until well mixed. Reduce the speed to low and blend in flour mixture.

INTO THE OVEN Roll the dough into 1¼-inch balls. Place 2 inches apart on ungreased cookie sheets. Flatten the balls slightly and press an almond into the center of each cookie. Beat the egg yolk and water together in a cup and brush on cookies. Bake for 11 to 15 minutes, until just set. Transfer the cookies to wire racks to cool completely.

Makes 4 dozen cookies

Per cookie: 80 calories, 1g protein, 8g carbohydrates, 5g fat, 3g saturated fat, 20mg cholesterol, 55mg sodium

Banana Snack Bars, page 42

Best of the Bars

When you want cookies fast, bake up one of our bars. These are not only speedy, but easy, too. Just pull out a baking pan, reach for your mixing bowl, and pick out a favorite recipe from our collection. The best of the best are here—from hi-carb energy bars to raspberry cream cheese bars and the richest brownies ever. Zap a quick peanut butter bar in the microwave, stir up a fruity bar with blueberries, bake up some tangy lemon bars. You'll find the fastest and safest way to get the bars out of the pan, and even learn what shortbreads and petticoats have in common. Plus how to turn your favorite drop cookie recipe into a delicious bar. Start baking a batch of bars right now to find your "best of the best."

SuperQuick

FRUITY CARB BARS

Prep **15 MINUTES**   _Microwave_ **2 MINUTES**

1   **cup light corn syrup**

1   **cup sugar**

¾   **cup reduced-fat peanut butter**

4   **cups grape nuts cereal**

1   **cup dried fruit, such as raisins, cranberries, or cherries, or dried fruit bits**

Grape nuts cereal has a crunch that will have you coming back for more. Be sure to really pack the mixture into the pan.

LET'S BEGIN Line a 13×9-inch pan with foil and spray lightly with nonstick cooking spray. Mix the corn syrup, sugar, and peanut butter together in a large microwavable bowl.

MICROWAVE & MIX Microwave on High for 2 minutes, or just until the mixture boils, stirring every minute. Stir in the cereal and dried fruit until coated.

ROLL & CUT Press the mixture firmly into the pan. When cool, cut into bars.

**Makes 30 bars**

Per bar: 150 calories, 3g protein, 30g carbohydrates, 3g fat, 1g saturated fat, 0mg cholesterol, 150mg sodium

SuperQuick

BANANA SNACK BARS

Prep **15 MINUTES**   _Bake_ **12 MINUTES**

1   **package (15½ ounces) banana nut-crunch cereal**

½   **cup all-purpose flour**

⅔   **cup honey**

6   **tablespoons butter or margarine**

When that mid-morning slump hits, reach for one of these treats.

LET'S BEGIN Preheat the oven to 350°F. Line a 13×9-inch baking pan with foil. Butter the foil. Mix the cereal and flour together in a large bowl.

BLEND IT IN Bring the honey and butter to boil in a small saucepan over medium-high heat, stirring constantly. Pour over the cereal mixture and stir until well coated. Press the mixture firmly into the pan with moistened fingers.

INTO THE OVEN Bake for 12 to 15 minutes, until light brown. Transfer to a wire rack to cool. Cut into bars.

**Makes 16 bars**

Per bar: 214 calories, 3g protein, 35g carbohydrates, 7g fat, 3g saturated fat, 12mg cholesterol, 159mg sodium

Fruity Carb Bars

SUNFLOWER & CRANBERRY GRANOLA BARS

Prep **15 MINUTES**   *Bake* **25 MINUTES**

1½   cups quick-cooking
      oats

¼   cup salted sunflower
      kernels + more for
      sprinkling (optional)

½   cup coconut + more for
      sprinkling (optional)

½   cup dried cranberries

¼   cup toasted wheat germ

¼   cup whole-wheat flour

¼   teaspoon ground
      cinnamon

½   teaspoon ground nutmeg

½   cup sunflower margarine

½   cup packed brown sugar

½   cup honey

Making granola has never been easier—or more delicious! This one-bowl version is packed with all that is delicious.

LET'S BEGIN Preheat the oven to 350°F. For the oat mixture, mix the first eight ingredients together in a large bowl.

POUR & PRESS Melt the margarine in a medium saucepan and stir in the brown sugar and honey. Bring to a boil, then pour over the oat mixture. Stir until coated. Press the mixture into a buttered 8-inch square baking pan. Sprinkle with extra sunflower kernels and coconut, if you like.

INTO THE OVEN Bake for 25 to 30 minutes, until light brown around the edges. While the bars are warm, press the surface gently with the back of a spoon to flatten. Score into bars with a knife. Cool completely, then cut into bars.

Makes 2 dozen bars

Per bar: 128 calories, 2g protein, 8g carbohydrates, 6g fat, 2g saturated fat, 0mg cholesterol, 64mg sodium

WHOLESOME GRANOLA BARS

Prep **15 MINUTES**   *Bake* **20 MINUTES**

1½   cups low-fat granola

1   cup quick or old-fashioned oats

¾   cup dried tart cherries

½   cup all-purpose flour

⅓   cup slivered almonds, toasted

½   teaspoon ground cinnamon

2   large egg whites, lightly beaten

⅓   cup honey

¼   cup packed brown sugar

2   tablespoons vegetable oil

These chock-full-of-goodness bars are great tasting and good for you, too. They make the perfect take-along breakfast.

LET'S BEGIN Preheat the oven to 350°F. Line an 8-inch square baking pan with foil. Lightly spray the foil with nonstick cooking spray and set aside.

INTO THE BOWL Toss the first six ingredients in a large bowl. Stir the remaining ingredients together in a small bowl. Stir into the cereal mixture until coated. Press into the pan.

INTO THE OVEN Bake for 20 to 25 minutes, until the bars are light brown. Transfer to a wire rack to cool. Lift the bars out of the pan. Cool completely, then cut into bars.

Makes 20 bars

Per bar: 120 calories, 2g protein, 22g carbohydrates, 3g fat, 0g saturated fat, 0mg cholesterol, 24mg sodium

SHAPE THEM YOUR WAY!

PLAIN & FANCY

If you have a shallow earthenware shortbread mold, by all means use it. Its decorative design transfers to the cookies. (If you don't have a mold, a pie plate works fine.) Use our Maple-Butter Pecan Shortbread recipe. Forget the topping and bake just until the shortbread starts to brown around the edge and the center is firm and golden, about 25 minutes. Cut into wedges.

LOG & SLICE

To make decorative rounds of shortbread, prepare the shortbread dough, omitting the topping. Shape it into a log, about 1½ inches in diameter. Chill until firm. Cut into ¼-inch-thick slices and place them on greased cookie sheets. Make a crosshatch design with a fork.

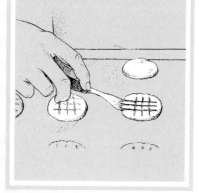

MAPLE-BUTTER PECAN SHORTBREAD

Prep **10 MINUTES**   *Bake* **32 MINUTES**

Shortbread dough made with brown sugar has a special homey quality. The maple syrup–pecan topping will have you coming back for more. A food processor makes quick work of chopping the nuts.

½	cup butter, softened
⅔	cup packed brown sugar
1	cup all-purpose flour
3	tablespoons pure maple syrup
1	large egg
½	cup finely chopped pecans

LET'S BEGIN Preheat the oven to 350°F. Combine the butter and ⅓ cup of the brown sugar in a small bowl. Beat with an electric mixer on medium speed until creamy. Reduce the speed to low and add the flour. Beat until a dough forms.

INTO THE OVEN Press the dough evenly into an ungreased 8-inch square baking pan. Prick the dough all over with a fork. Bake the cookies for 20 minutes.

TOP & BAKE Combine the remaining ⅓ cup of brown sugar, the maple syrup, and egg in a small bowl and mix well. Spread the topping over the hot shortbread and sprinkle with the pecans. Bake for 12 to 16 minutes more, until light brown. Immediately run a knife around edges of the shortbread to loosen. Cool completely. Cut into bars.

Makes 25 bars

Per bar: 100 calories, 1g protein, 12g carbohydrates, 6g fat, 3g saturated fat, 20mg cholesterol, 45mg sodium

RASPBERRY SHORTBREAD BARS

Prep **20 MINUTES + COOLING** *Bake* **30 MINUTES**

DOUGH

1½   cups all-purpose flour

½   cup sugar

1   cup quick-cooking or old-fashioned oats

½   teaspoon baking soda

¼   teaspoon salt

¾   cup butter

FILLING

1   tablespoon cornstarch

1   tablespoon water

1   package (10 ounces) frozen deluxe red raspberries, thawed

You can use either quick-cooking or old-fashioned oats for this recipe with great success. It simply depends upon how much crunch you prefer and what you have on hand.

LET'S BEGIN Preheat the oven to 350°F. Grease a 9-inch square baking pan. To make the dough, combine the first five ingredients in a large bowl and cut in the butter until crumbly. Reserve ¾ cup of the crumb mixture for the topping. Press the remaining crumb mixture into the pan.

BUBBLE & SPREAD To make the filling, stir the cornstarch and water in a small saucepan until blended. Add the raspberries and cook, stirring, over medium heat for 5 minutes, or until thick and smooth. Cool. Spread raspberries over the crust and sprinkle with the reserved crumb mixture.

INTO THE OVEN Bake for 30 minutes, or until the edges are light brown. Cool completely before cutting into bars.

Makes 2 dozen bars
Per bar: 120 calories, 1g protein, 15g carbohydrates, 6g fat, 4g saturated fat, 15mg cholesterol, 135mg sodium

Food Facts

SHORTBREAD & PETTICOAT TAILS

In the land of the shortbread in Scotland, these cherished, buttery-rich cookies were once served only during Christmas and Hogmanay (the Scottish New Year's Eve). Shortbread was baked in a round wooden mold, which was decoratively carved and notched around the edge to signify the sun's rays. The dough was pressed into the mold and turned out onto a cookie sheet, then baked and cut into wedges. The cookies were named petticoat tails for their shape, resembling the bell-hoop petticoats worn by court ladies in the 12th century.

RASPBERRY & CREAM CHEESE BARS

Prep **15 MINUTES**   *Bake* **22 MINUTES**

CRUST

1½   cups all-purpose flour

⅓   cup sugar

⅓   cup unsalted butter or margarine, softened

¼   cup cream cheese, softened

1   large egg, lightly beaten

¼   teaspoon almond extract

TOPPING

1   cup raspberry preserves

¾   cup cream cheese, softened

¼   cup sugar

2   tablespoons milk

To soften cream cheese to room temperature, put it in a bowl of hot tap water for a few minutes while it's still in its foil wrapper.

LET'S BEGIN Preheat the oven to 375°F. Butter a 13 × 9-inch baking pan. To make the crust, mix the flour and sugar in a medium bowl. Blend in the butter and cream cheese until the mixture resembles coarse crumbs. Add the egg and almond extract, stirring until a dough forms.

INTO THE OVEN Press the dough into the pan. Bake for 12 to 14 minutes, until the edges are light brown.

DECORATE Spread the raspberry preserves on top. To make the topping, mix the cream cheese, sugar, and milk in a bowl. Drop by teaspoonfuls over the raspberry preserves. Run a knife lightly through topping to create swirls. Bake for 10 to 12 minutes, until set. Cool completely, then cut into bars.

Makes 30 bars

Per bar: 116 calories, 1g protein, 16g carbohydrates, 5g fat, 3g saturated fat, 21mg cholesterol, 27mg sodium

ROCKY ROAD BROWNIES

Prep **20 MINUTES**   *Bake* **33 MINUTES**

BROWNIES

½   cup butter or margarine

3   ounces (3 squares) unsweetened chocolate

1   cup all-purpose flour

¾   teaspoon baking powder

½   teaspoon salt

3   large eggs

1½ cups sugar

1½ teaspoons vanilla extract

TOPPING

½   cup chopped peanuts

½   cup semisweet chocolate chips

½   cup miniature marshmallows

¼   cup chocolate fudge topping, warmed

These rocky-road brownies are over the top. They are made with chocolate, chocolate chips, and chocolate fudge topping, making them triple-delicious—and reminiscent of the sundaes we all love.

LET'S BEGIN Preheat the oven to 350°F. Butter a 9-inch square baking pan. To make the brownies, melt the butter and unsweetened chocolate in a medium saucepan over low heat, stirring frequently. Set aside to cool. Combine the flour, baking powder, and salt in a small bowl.

INTO THE BOWL Beat the eggs in a large bowl until frothy. Add the sugar, 2 tablespoons at a time, beating until the mixture is thick, then add the vanilla. Beat in the chocolate mixture until blended, then stir in the flour mixture just until blended. Spread evenly in the pan.

INTO THE OVEN Bake for 25 to 30 minutes, until the edges slightly pull away from the sides of the pan. To top, sprinkle with the peanuts, chocolate chips, and marshmallows, then drizzle with chocolate fudge topping. Bake for 8 to 12 minutes more, or until light brown. Transfer to a wire rack and cool completely. Cut into bars.

Makes 2 dozen bars
Per bar: 175 calories, 3g protein, 23g carbohydrates, 9g fat, 5g saturated fat, 37mg cholesterol, 128mg sodium

---

Food Facts

HOW THE BROWNIE GOT ITS NAME

The name of this cake-like cookie called a *brownie* comes from its deep brown color. Americans have been in love with the brownie ever since it first appeared in print in Fannie Farmer's *The Original Boston Cooking-School Cook Book*, 1906. Many versions of the brownie exist, including the Rocky Road, based upon the chocolate confection of milk or dark chocolate, marshmallows, and nuts.

Yummy Peanut Butter Bars

YUMMY PEANUT BUTTER BARS

Prep **10 MINUTES**   *Bake* **18 MINUTES**   *Microwave* **1 MINUTE**

1	package (17½ ounces) home-style peanut butter cookie mix
1	large egg
1	tablespoon water
⅓	cup chopped salted peanuts
3	tablespoons butter or margarine, softened
½	cup creamy home-style classic vanilla frosting
¼	cup semisweet chocolate chips
2	teaspoons vegetable shortening

Here, a fast peanut butter bar with double glazes, double the goodness, and triple the flavor.

LET'S BEGIN Preheat the oven to 350°F. Combine the cookie mix, peanut butter packet (from the mix), egg, and water in a large bowl. Stir in the peanuts then spread in an 8-inch square baking pan. Bake for 18 to 20 minutes, until the edges are light golden. Transfer to a wire rack to cool.

GLAZE & SET To make the glazes, spoon the frosting into a small microwavable bowl and combine the chocolate and shortening in a cup. Microwave each on High for 10 to 30 seconds, until the frosting is soft and the chocolate mixture melts. Drizzle the glazes over the bars.

Makes 2 dozen bars
Per bar: 152 calories, 2g protein, 20g carbohydrates, 7g fat, 2g saturated fat, 13mg cholesterol, 142mg sodium

ZAP-IT BARS

Prep **14 MINUTES**   *Microwave* **1 MINUTE**

½	cup packed brown sugar
½	cup honey
½	cup peanut butter
3	cups spoon-size shredded-wheat cereal, coarsely crushed
¾	cup raisins
½	cup chopped unsalted dry-roasted peanuts

A super-speedy peanut bar cookie! Try substituting for the raisins: dried cherries, dried cranberries, or chopped, dried apricots.

LET'S BEGIN Put sugar, honey, and peanut butter in microwavable bowl. Microwave on High for 1 minute, or until bubbly. Stir until blended, then add remaining ingredients.

SHAPE & CUT Firmly press into a buttered 8-inch square baking pan. Cool. Cut into 24 bars (2 × 1¼ inches).

Makes 2 dozen bars
Per bar: 115 calories, 3g protein, 19g carbohydrates, 4g fat, 1g saturated fat, 0mg cholesterol, 28mg sodium

BLUEBERRY STREUSEL SQUARES

Prep **15 MINUTES**   *Bake* **33 MINUTES**

1½   **cups quick or old fashioned oats**

1¼   **cups all-purpose flour**

1½   **cup packed brown sugar**

¾   **cup margarine or butter, melted**

1   **cup fresh or frozen blueberries (do not thaw)**

⅓   **cup raspberry preserves**

1   **teaspoon all-purpose flour**

½   **teaspoon grated lemon zest**

Think of this sweet as a fabulous crumb pie without all the work. The combination of fresh blueberries and raspberry jam makes a filling that has lots of rich fruit flavor and a tempting texture.

LET'S BEGIN Preheat the oven to 350°F. Mix the oats, flour, brown sugar, and margarine together until crumbly. Set aside 1 cup of the oat mixture. Press the remainder onto the bottom of an ungreased 8- or 9-inch baking pan. Bake for 13 to 15 minutes, until light golden. Cool slightly.

MIX IT UP Meanwhile, gently stir the blueberries, preserves, flour, and lemon zest together in a medium bowl. Spread over the crust then sprinkle the reserved oat mixture on top, patting it gently.

INTO THE OVEN Bake for 20 to 22 minutes, until light golden brown. Cool completely then cut into squares.

Makes 16 squares

Per square: 190 calories, 2g protein, 25g carbohydrates, 9g fat, 2g saturated fat, 0mg cholesterol, 105mg sodium

CHUNKY CHOCOLATE BLONDE BROWNIES

Prep **20 MINUTES**   *Bake* **25 MINUTES**

1½   cups all-purpose flour

1   teaspoon baking soda

½   teaspoon salt

1¼   cups butter, softened

¾   cup packed brown sugar

½   cup granulated sugar

1   large egg

1   teaspoon vanilla extract

1⅔   cups quick or old-fashioned oats

1¾   cups semisweet chocolate chunks

Here is the best of both worlds. A blonde brownie that has chunks of semisweet chocolate. Use the best quality chocolate you can find.

LET'S BEGIN Preheat the oven to 375°F. Combine the flour, baking soda, and salt in a medium bowl.

INTO THE BOWL Beat the butter, brown sugar, and granulated sugar in a large bowl with a wooden spoon until creamy. Beat in the egg and vanilla. Stir in the flour mixture until well blended, then stir in the oats and 1 cup of the chocolate chunks.

INTO THE OVEN Spread the dough evenly in an ungreased 13 × 9-inch pan. Bake for 25 to 30 minutes, until light golden. Transfer to a wire rack and sprinkle with the remaining chocolate chunks. Let stand for 2 minutes. Evenly spread softened chocolate on top. Cool and cut into bars.

Makes 2 dozen bars
Per bar: 244 calories, 2g protein, 28g carbohydrates, 15g fat, 9g saturated fat, 36mg cholesterol, 211mg sodium

---

Time Savers

LIFT BARS OUT OF THE PAN—FAST

When making bar cookies, slicing them up and getting them out of the pan into neat, even bars is often the most frustrating and time-consuming part.

Here's a quick baker's tip: Line the pan with foil, leaving a 1-inch overhang on all sides. Grease the bottom and sides of the foil (not the overhang, please!) with shortening and put in the cookie dough. When the bars are done, let them rest in the pan for 5 minutes, then lift them out, foil and all, onto a wire rack. Cool them completely, then slice into bars, right on the foil.

CHOCOLATE CHIP CARAMEL BARS

Prep **15 MINUTES**   *Bake* **35 MINUTES**

1   bag (14 ounces) caramels, unwrapped

1   can (4 ounces) evaporated milk

1   package (17½ ounces) chocolate chip cookie mix

1   large egg

2   tablespoons water

5   tablespoons vegetable oil

Unwrapping caramels is just the job for little hands. And the reward is these decadently delicious (and easy) bar cookies!

LET'S BEGIN Preheat the oven to 375°F. Spray an 8-inch square baking pan with nonstick cooking spray. Melt caramels and evaporated milk in a small saucepan over low heat.

STIR & SPREAD Prepare the cookie mix according to package directions. Press two-thirds of the dough into the pan.

INTO THE OVEN Bake for 15 to 18 minutes, until golden brown. Gently pour the caramel over the bottom crust. Drop heaping teaspoonfuls of the remaining cookie dough over the caramel. Bake for 20 to 25 minutes, until golden brown and set in the center. Transfer the pan to a wire rack to cool completely, then cut into bars.

Makes 15 bars

Per bar: 320 calories, 4g protein, 43g carbohydrates, 16g fat, 5g saturated fat, 18mg cholesterol, 173mg sodium

---

Time Savers

FAST-BAKE DROP COOKIES IN BARS

Dropping cookies one by one onto cookie sheets is one of the most time-consuming parts of baking cookies. If you're short on time, just scrap the dough into a buttered baking pan.

For cake-like cookies: Use a 8- or 9-inch square pan for 8 ounces of cookie dough (about 3 cups), or a 13x9-inch pan for 1 pound of cookie dough (about 6 cups). Bake at the temperature given in the recipe for about 25 minutes, or until set in the center.

For slice 'n' bake cookies, form the drop cookie dough into a log about 1½ inches in diameter and refrigerate or freeze. Then, just slice and bake at the temperature in the recipe.

BROWN SUGAR & APPLE BARS

Prep **25 MINUTES**   *Bake* **20 MINUTE**

1   cup all-purpose flour

2   teaspoons ground cinnamon

1   teaspoon baking soda

½   teaspoon ground cloves

½   cup unsalted butter or margarine, softened

1   cup packed brown sugar

1   large egg

11   medium apple, peeled, cored, and coarsely shredded

Brown-Sugar Frosting (see recipe)

½   cup chopped nuts (optional)

The taste and aroma of autumn is in these irresistible bar cookies. For the most flavor use a tasty apple, such as a McIntosh, Fuji, or other sweet-tart variety.

LET'S BEGIN Preheat the oven to 350°F. Butter an 8-inch square baking pan. Combine the flour, cinnamon, baking soda, and cloves in a small bowl.

BEAT & SPREAD Beat the butter and brown sugar in a large bowl with a wooden spoon until light and fluffy. Beat in the egg until well blended. Stir in the flour mixture until well blended, then stir in the apple. Spread evenly in the pan.

INTO THE OVEN Bake for 20 to 25 minutes, until a wooden pick inserted in the center comes out clean. Transfer to a wire rack to cool completely. Make the Brown-Sugar Frosting. Frost the cooled bars and sprinkle with nuts, if you like.

BROWN-SUGAR FROSTING

Put 1¾ cups confectioners' sugar, 4 ounces softened cream cheese, ¼ cup softened unsalted butter or margarine, and ¼ cup packed light brown sugar in a large bowl. Stir until smooth.

Makes 2 dozen
Per bar: 162 calories, 1g protein, 25g carbohydrates, 7g fat, 4g saturated fat, 27mg cholesterol, 75mg sodium

CARAMEL PINEAPPLE BAR COOKIES

Prep **15 MINUTES** + **COOLING**   *Bake* **20 MINUTES**

2	cups all-purpose flour
1½	cups quick-cooking or old-fashioned oats
1	teaspoon baking soda
½	cup margarine or butter, softened
1	cup packed brown sugar
2	large eggs
2	tablespoons milk
1	teaspoon vanilla extract
1	can (20 ounces) pineapple tidbits or crushed pineapple, well drained
½	cup caramel ice cream topping

The easiest and neatest way to cut through these bar cookies is to use an up-and-down sawing motion. If you lightly oil the knife, the cookies won't stick to it. Be sure to thoroughly drain the pineapple.

LET'S BEGIN Preheat the oven to 350°F. Grease and flour a 13 × 9-inch baking pan. Combine the flour, oats, and baking soda in a medium bowl.

STIR IT IN Beat the margarine and brown sugar until light and fluffy in a medium bowl. Stir in the eggs, milk, and vanilla until well combined. Gradually stir in the flour mixture until thoroughly mixed. Add the pineapple and stir until just mixed. Spread evenly in the pan.

INTO THE OVEN Bake for 20 to 25 minutes, until a wooden pick inserted in center comes out clean. Cool for 15 minutes. Drizzle caramel sauce over the top and cut into bars.

Makes 2 dozen bars
Per bar: 158 calories, 2g protein, 26g carbohydrates, 5g fat, 1g saturated fat, 18mg cholesterol, 131mg sodium

---

Baking Basics

MAKE A FAST COOKIE PARFAIT!

Turn these Caramel Pineapple Bar Cookies into elegant dessert parfaits. If you have parfait glasses, use them. If not, choose any clear tall glasses, preferably stemmed ones. Toast some chopped pecans. Break a few of the bars into small bite-size pieces. Set out some vanilla ice cream to soften a little. Right before serving time, layer up the parfaits: a spoonful of ice cream, 1 or 2 pieces of the cookie bars, some caramel topping, a few pecans. Repeat until the glass is full, ending with the pecans. Top each parfait with a small paper umbrella.

DOUBLE-LEMON BARS

Prep **20 MINUTES + CHILLING**   *Bake* **32 MINUTES**

CRUST

⅓   cup butter, softened

⅓   cup sugar

1   cup all-purpose flour

FILLING

¾   cup sugar

3   tablespoons all-purpose flour

½   teaspoon baking powder

⅛   teaspoon salt

1   tablespoon grated lemon zest

2   tablespoons lemon juice

2   large eggs

TOPPING

Confectioners' sugar

White decorator's icing (see page 133, optional)

Calling all lemon lovers! When grating lemon, grate only the flavorful colored part of the peel (the zest). The white pith is bitter.

LET'S BEGIN Preheat the oven to 350°F. Line an 8- or 9-inch square baking pan with foil, leaving a 1-inch overhang. Lightly butter the pan. To make the crust, beat all of the crust ingredients in a small bowl with an electric mixer on medium speed until well mixed. Press onto the bottom of the pan. Bake for 15 to 17 minutes, until the edges begin to brown.

MIX IT UP Meanwhile, beat all of the filling ingredients in the same bowl with an electric mixer on medium speed until light. Pour the filling over the hot crust. Bake for 17 to 20 minutes longer, until the top is light golden brown.

DECORATE Dust top of bars with the confectioners' sugar. Cool on wire rack in pan. Lift the bars out of the pan using the overhanging foil as handles. Peel foil away from the sides of the bars. Cut into 20 bars (2 × 1½ × 2 inches). Decorate with a swirl of white icing, if you like. Refrigerate until ready to serve.

Makes 20 bars

Per bar: 58 calories, 1g protein, 9g carbohydrates, 2g fat, 1g saturated fat, 17mg cholesterol, 35mg sodium

Cook to Cook

HOW CAN I GRATE A LEMON FAST?

" I have this amazing new type of grater—it's called *a microplane grater-zester.* It has an 8-inch blade with razor sharp edges and a comfortable fat grip. It *makes fast work out of grating the* *zest of a lemon or orange.* It's just the thing to grate hard cheeses and chocolate, too. Look for other microplane graters: a spice grater and a ribbon grater for apples and soft cheeses. "

Our Very Best Brownies

Prep **20 MINUTES + COOLING**   *Bake* **30 MINUTES**

BROWNIES

½   cup all-purpose flour

⅓   cup unsweetened cocoa

¼   teaspoon baking powder

¼   teaspoon salt

½   cup butter or margarine, melted

1   cup granulated sugar

1   teaspoon vanilla extract

2   large eggs

½   cup chopped nuts (optional)

CREAMY BROWNIE FROSTING

3   tablespoons butter or margarine, softened

3   tablespoons unsweetened cocoa

1   tablespoon light corn syrup or honey

½   teaspoon vanilla extract

1   cup confectioners' sugar

2   tablespoons milk

Here's the fudgy-est, richest, most delicious brownie ever, complete with a layer of creamy fudge frosting on top. Turn it into a sundae with a scoop of vanilla ice cream and a drizzle of fudge sauce.

LET'S BEGIN Preheat the oven to 350°F. Stir the flour, cocoa, baking powder, and salt in a medium bowl. Set aside.

MIX IT IN Stir the butter, granulated sugar, and vanilla in a large bowl until creamy. Beat in the eggs, then the flour mixture until well blended. Stir in the nuts, if you like. Spread the batter evenly in a buttered 9-inch square baking pan.

INTO THE OVEN Bake for 20 to 25 minutes, until the brownies begin to pull away from sides of pan. Cool completely in pan on wire rack. Meanwhile, beat the butter, cocoa, corn syrup, and vanilla in a small bowl. Beat in the confectioners' sugar and milk until the frosting is of spreading consistency. Spread over the cooled brownies. Cut into squares or bars.

Makes 16 brownies
Per brownie: 185 calories, 2g protein, 25g carbohydrates, 9g fat, 6g saturated fat, 49mg cholesterol, 140mg sodium

CARAMEL-PECAN BROWNIES

Prep **20 MINUTES**   *Bake* **30 MINUTES**

1½ cups all-purpose flour

1   teaspoon baking powder

½   teaspoon salt

8   ounces semisweet chocolate

¾   cup unsalted butter or margarine

½   cups granulated sugar

3   large eggs

2   teaspoons vanilla

1   cup coarsely chopped pecans

16 caramels, unwrapped

1   tablespoon milk

This combination of chocolate, pecans, and caramel is a classic. They are sometimes called turtle brownies because they are reminiscent of turtle candies.

LET'S BEGIN Preheat the oven to 350°F. Butter a 13×9-inch baking pan. Stir the flour, baking powder, and salt together in a small bowl and set aside. Combine the chocolate and butter in a large saucepan and cook over low heat until melted, stirring occasionally. Remove from heat.

MIX IT UP Add the sugar and mix well. Add the eggs, one at a time, beating well after each addition. Stir in the vanilla. Blend in the flour mixture. Spread it in the pan and sprinkle with the pecans. Combine the caramels and milk in a small saucepan. Cook over low heat until the caramels melt, stirring constantly. Pour the caramel mixture over the pecans.

BAKE & CUT Bake brownies for 30 minutes or until edges pull away slightly from pan. Cool completely. Cut into bars.

Makes 30 bars
Per bar: 184 calories, 2g protein, 23g carbohydrates, 10g fat, 5g saturated fat, 34mg cholesterol, 60mg sodium

---

Baking Basics

HAVE-IT-YOUR-WAY BROWNIES

Start with your favorite brownie recipe, then mix and bake them the way you like best.
For light cake-like brownies, add an extra egg and beat the batter with an electric mixer on high until it forms a flat ribbon. Lift the beater and the batter will fall back on itself. Bake brownies until a toothpick inserted halfway between the side of pan and the center comes out clean.
For brownies with a ultra-smooth texture, use cake flour instead of all-purpose flour.
For extra-fudgy brownies, add an extra egg, but beat the batter only a minute or two, just until the ingredients are blended. Start checking for doneness 5 to 10 minutes before end of bake time. Bake only until a toothpick inserted halfway between side of pan and center comes out almost clean.

Little Ladies, page 70

Kids in the Kitchen

Cooking with the kids is fun, especially when the recipes are easy, fast, and kid-proof—and that's exactly what you'll find here. Expect the unexpected in our collection: ladybugs you can eat, lollipops you bake, S'mores you don't need a campfire to make. All come with kid-pleasing ingredients and names, such as Oodle-Kadoodles and Peanut Gobblers. You'll find cookies to send to school, others to cheer up a rainy day, and a couple guaranteed to make a hit at that next birthday party. We've tucked in cookies just made for little helping hands. All are mixed in minutes and baked in a few, plus some are not even baked at all. And every one is guaranteed to turn out to be a winner.

GUM DROP COOKIES

Prep **30 MINUTES + CHILLING**   *Bake* **10 MINUTES**

- 2 cups all-purpose flour
- 1 cup quick-cooking oats
- 1 teaspoon baking soda
- ½ teaspoon salt
- ½ cup butter, softened
- 1 cup granulated sugar
- ¼ cup packed brown sugar
- 2 large eggs
- 1 teaspoon vanilla extract
- 1 cup chopped gum drops

Gumdrops and kids just go together. Let the kids help make the dough by snipping the gum drops with scissors and shaping the logs.

LET'S BEGIN For the flour mixture, combine the first four ingredients. Beat butter and both sugars in a medium bowl with an electric mixer on medium speed until creamy. Beat in eggs and vanilla. Reduce the speed and blend in flour mixture.

MIX & SHAPE Stir in the gum drops by hand. Shape the dough into two $9 \times 1\frac{1}{2}$-inch logs and wrap each in waxed paper. Refrigerate for 2 hours, or until firm.

SLICE & BAKE Preheat oven to 350°F. Grease 2 cookie sheets. Cut the logs into ⅜-inch-thick slices with a serrated knife. Place 1 inch apart on cookie sheets. Bake for 10 minutes, or until light brown. Transfer to wire racks to cool.

Makes 4 dozen cookies

Per cookie: 80 calories, 1g protein, 14g carbohydrates, 3g fat, 1g saturated fat, 15mg cholesterol, 75mg sodium

RUBY COWBOY COOKIES

Prep **30 MINUTES + CHILLING**   *Bake* **13 MINUTES**

2   **rolls (18 ounces each) refrigerated sugar cookie dough**

½   **cup finely chopped walnuts**

1   **can cherry fruit filling or topping**

½   **cup confectioners' sugar**

Kids love to make thumbprint cookies—and these are the easiest ever. Refrigerated sugar cookie dough and pie filling are the secrets.

LET'S BEGIN Remove the dough from the package and allow to sit at room temperature for 30 minutes. Mix in the nuts with your hands. Cover and refrigerate for 1 hour.

DROP & BAKE Preheat oven to 350°F. Shape the dough into 24 balls and place on ungreased cookie sheets. Flatten slightly with your hands. Make an indentation in the middle of each with your thumb and fill with pie filling. Bake for 13 to 17 minutes. Transfer to wire racks and cool for 10 minutes.

DECORATE Cover the filling with an upside-down spoon while you dust the rest of the cookie with confectioners' sugar.

Makes 2 dozen cookies

Per cookie: 230 calories, 2g protein, 34g carbohydrates, 10g fat, 3g saturated fat, 10mg cholesterol, 190mg sodium

---

Cook to Cook

WHAT ARE SOME TIPS FOR COOKING WITH THE KIDS?

"First of all, *plan ahead!* Pick out the recipe together, making sure there's plenty for each child to do "on their own," whatever their age. Let the kids go shopping with you too, asking them to pick out "fun" things, such as the decorations for the cookies. Give each child a special task.

Think safety! Keep the cooking session safe, at all times. If there's chocolate or butter to be melted, let the kids help by using the microwavee. If not, assign this to a older child or do it yourself. The same goes for using knives, stirring hot pots, or taking cookie sheets in and out of a hot oven.

Give kids some creative control! Kids love to do things with their hands. So let them: stir the cookie dough, help drop the cookies or roll up the balls of dough, sprinkle nuts or coconut on bar cookies before they're baked, cut out sugar cookies in fun shapes and decorate them however they like, paint the baked sugar cookies with icing, help roll baked cookie balls in confectioners' sugar, or dip baked cookies in melted chocolate.

Be sure each child makes something. Nothing is more special than for each kid to be able to say "Would you like one? I made this myself!""

LOLLIPOP COOKIES

Prep **30 MINUTES**   *Bake* **12 MINUTES**

2   **extra-ripe medium bananas**

1½   **cups quick-cooking oats**

1½   **cups all-purpose flour**

1   **teaspoon ground cinnamon**

½   **teaspoon baking soda**

½   **teaspoon salt**

¾   **cup light butter or margarine**

¾   **cup packed brown sugar**

1   **large egg**

½   **teaspoon vanilla extract**

1½   **cups seedless raisins**

2   **dozen large wooden pop sticks (optional)**

All the flavors a kid could loves rolled into one fabulous cookie. The wooden pop sticks are found in craft stores.

LET'S BEGIN Preheat the oven to 350°F. Spray 2 cookie sheets with nonstick cooking spray. Purée the bananas in a blender. Combine the oats, flour, cinnamon, baking soda, and salt in a medium bowl.

BLEND IT IN Beat the margarine and the sugar with an electric mixer on medium speed in a large bowl. Beat in the egg, banana purée, and vanilla. Stir in the oat mixture until well blended, then add the raisins.

INTO THE OVEN Drop the dough by rounded table-spoonfuls 2 inches apart on cookie sheets. Flatten the tops with the back of a spoon. Insert a wooden stick into the side of each cookie to resemble a lollipop, if you like. Bake for 12 to 15 minutes, until light brown. Cool.

Makes 2 dozen cookies

Per cookie: 128 calories, 2g protein, 24g carbohydrates, 4g fat, 1g saturated fat, 9mg cholesterol, 109mg sodium

---

Baking Basics

4 COOKIE BAKING TIPS FOR KIDS

1. To make cookies the same size, drop batter with a small ice cream scoop (about 1½ inches in diameter). Spray the scoop first with nonstick spray.

2. To keep cookie dough from sticking to your hand, dip your hands periodically in a bowl of ice water, washing off any dough.

3. When flattening cookies with a fork or spoon, dip it often in a bowl of ice water. This keeps the dough from sticking to it.

4. To remove cookies that are stuck to a cookie sheet, ask an adult to put it on top of a pan of simmering water or put it on a hot, moistened towel.

PEANUT GOBBLERS

Prep **15 MINUTES**   *Bake* **8 MINUTES**

1   cup creamy or super-
    chunk peanut butter

1   cup sugar

1   egg, slightly beaten

1   teaspoon vanilla extract

**Sprinkles, chocolate chips,
chocolate candies (optional)**

*Creating the classic crisscross pattern in these extra-chunky,
peanut-y cookies is great fun for kids in the kitchen.*

LET'S BEGIN Preheat the oven to 325°F. Combine all of
the ingredients in a medium bowl.

ROLL & CUT Shape the dough into 1-inch balls. Arrange
the cookies 2 inches apart on ungreased cookie sheets. With
a fork, gently flatten each cookie (see below) and press a
crisscross pattern into the top with a fork.

INTO THE OVEN for 8 minutes, or until light brown and
slightly puffed. Immediately top, if desired, with sprinkles,
chocolate chips, or chocolate candies. Cool completely on
wire rack before removing from baking sheets.

Makes 2 dozen cookies

*Per cookie: 98 calories, 3g protein, 10g carbohydrates, 6g fat,
1g saturated fat, 9mg cholesterol, 53mg sodium*

Baking Basics

5 SIMPLE WAYS TO MAKE DROP COOKIES FLAT & CRISP

Start with your favorite cookie
dough, then follow these steps to
make cookies extra thin and crisp.

1. Increase the white sugar in the
dough by 1 to 2 tablespoons. If the
recipe has brown sugar, decrease it
by 1 tablespoon.

2. Grease the cookie sheets, even
if the recipe doesn't ask you to.

3. If the recipe calls for cold dough
(such as in slice & bake cookies),

chill it only until it's firm enough
to handle. Don't let it get too solid.

4. Flatten out each cookie gently,
using the bottom of a small water
glass. If the dough sticks to the

glass, dip the bottom in a little
flour. Press each cookie gently, not
too hard!

5. When the cookies are done, let
them rest on the cookie sheet for
about 3 minutes (instead of 1
minute that many recipes suggest),
then transfer them to a wire rack to
cool completely before storing
them. Avoid stacking the cookies
on the rack, as the steam from one
cookie can soften another.

SuperQuick

CHERRY CHEWS

Prep **20 MINUTES**   *Bake* **10 MINUTES**

1½   cups all-purpose flour

1   teaspoon baking powder

½   teaspoon salt (optional)

1   cup butter or margarine, softened

1   cup firmly packed brown sugar

½   cup granulated sugar

2   large eggs

1   teaspoon vanilla extract

2   cups quick-cooking or old-fashioned oats

1½   cups dried tart cherries

1   cup semisweet chocolate chips

Chocolate, cherries, and kids simply go together. Dried tart cherries are actually sweet-tart in flavor, making them perfect in these cookies.

LET'S BEGIN Preheat the oven to 350°F. Combine the flour, baking powder, and salt and set aside. Put the butter and both of the sugars in a large bowl.

MIX IT UP Beat with an electric mixer on medium speed for 3 minutes, or until creamy. Add the eggs and vanilla and beat well. Blend in the flour mixture. Stir in the oats, cherries, and chocolate chips. Mix well.

INTO THE OVEN Drop the dough by rounded tablespoonfuls onto ungreased cookie sheets. Bake for 10 minutes, or until golden brown. Cool for 1 minute on cookie sheets, then transfer to wire rack to cool completely.

Makes 4 dozen cookies
Per cookie: 120 calories, 1g protein, 17g carbohydrates, 6g fat, 3g saturated fat, 20mg cholesterol, 55mg sodium

SuperQuick

LITTLE LADIES

Prep **20 MINUTES**

2 chocolate sandwich cookies

1 to 2 teaspoons ready-to-spread white frosting, tinted red

10 miniature semisweet chocolate chips

1 small red or black gum drop

Black shoestring licorice

Here are ladybugs that kids can eat! For they're made with store-bought chocolate sandwich cookies. This recipe makes one. If you wish, store up on the ingredients and make several.

LET'S BEGIN Pull 1 sandwich cookie apart. Set aside the plain round cookie (eat the frosted one). For wings, cut remaining sandwich cookie into 2 filled semicircles. Spread top sides with red frosting and press in chips for spots.

FROST IT FAST Secure the wings (frosted sides up and rounded edges out) with frosting to top of plain round cookie, separating wings slightly.

FINAL TOUCH Halve the gum drop horizontally; press cut ends together for head. Cut licorice into two (2-inch) pieces for antennae. Make 2 holes in head with toothpick; push antennae into holes. Secure head with frosting to body.

Makes 1 cookie

Per cookie: 143 calories, 1g protein, 24g carbohydrates, 5g fat, 2g saturated fat, 0mg cholesterol, 124mg sodium

APPLE-K-DABBERS

Prep **30 MINUTES**   *Bake* **10 MINUTES**

1½   cups old-fashioned or
      quick-cooking oats

¼   cup all-purpose flour

2   teaspoons cinnamon

½   teaspoon nutmeg

¼   teaspoon allspice

½   teaspoon baking powder

½   teaspoon salt

1   cup unsalted butter or
      margarine, softened

¾   cup firmly packed dark
      brown sugar

½   cup granulated sugar

1   large egg

1   cup peeled and chopped
      apples

These contain all of the warm spices of autumn: cinnamon, nutmeg, and allspice. For the best nutmeg flavor, buy whole nutmeg and grate just as much as you need on the small holes of a grater.

LET'S BEGIN Preheat the oven to 375°F. Lightly grease cookie sheets. For the flour mixture, mix the first seven ingredients in a medium bowl.

MIX IT IN Beat the butter and both sugars in a large bowl until light and fluffy. Add the egg and mix well. Stir in the flour mixture until well combined and mix in the apples.

DROP & BAKE Drop by rounded teaspoonfuls on cookie sheets. Bake for 10 to 12 minutes, until light brown around the edges. Transfer to wire rack to cool.

Makes 4 dozen cookies

Per cookie: 73 calories, 1g protein, 8g carbohydrates, 4g fat, 3g saturated fat, 15mg cholesterol, 32mg sodium

---

Cook to Cook

HOW CAN I TELL WHEN MY COOKIES ARE DONE?

❝ It's not easy to know when to take cookies out of the oven. Even the bake time for the same cookie recipe can vary from time to time. *It all depends on how hot your oven is* and where you put the pan. Check often and take out cookies that are done, leaving in the rest.

Like chewy cookies that are a little soft? Bake them a minute or two less than the time called for in the recipe.

Prefer crisp cookies? Then let the cookies bake a little longer than the recipe suggests. And be sure to cool them on a wire rack.

Take a test cookie about 5 minutes before the cookies should be done. It's time to take out the cookies when the edges are light brown and the centers look puffy and set. If your oven does not heat evenly, rotate and turn the cookie sheets once or twice. ❞

OODLE-KADOODLES

Prep **25 MINUTES**   *Microwave* **3 MINUTES**   *Chill* **40 MINUTES**

1	package (12 ounces) semisweet chocolate chips (2 cups)
1⅔	cups peanut butter chips
1¾	cups creamy or crunchy peanut butter
3	cups chow mein noodles
1	cup chopped peanuts
1	cup raisins

This unusual no-bake chocolate cookie turns out unexpectedly fast and delicious with the help of the microwave.

LET'S BEGIN Line cookie sheets with waxed paper. Place the first three ingredients in a large microwavable bowl.

COOK & STIR Microwave on High for 1 minute, then stir. Continue heating for 30 seconds at a time, checking and stirring, until chips are melted (watch carefully to prevent burning!). Stir in the noodles, peanuts, and raisins.

CHILL IT Drop cookies by heaping teaspoonfuls on the cookie sheets. Chill for 40 minutes to set. Store in refrigerator.

Makes about 4½ dozen

Per cookie: 158 calories, 5g protein, 14g carbohydrates, 10g fat, 4g saturated fat, 0mg cholesterol, 92mg sodium

SuperQuick
MMM-GOOD COOKIES

Prep **15 MINUTES**   *Bake* **9 MINUTES**

2½	cups all-purpose flour
1	teaspoon baking soda
1	cup butter or margarine
¾	cup sugar
¾	cup firmly packed brown sugar
2	large eggs
1	tablespoon vanilla
1	package (14 ounces) candy-coated chocolate pieces (2 cups)

No matter what's your name, it's hard to resist these little candy-coated chocolate bites.

LET'S BEGIN Preheat the oven to 375°F. Mix flour and baking soda and set aside. Beat all of the remaining ingredients except chocolate in a large bowl with an electric mixer on medium speed for 1 to 2 minutes, until creamy.

MIX IT IN Reduce the speed to low and blend in the flour mixture. Stir in the chocolate pieces by hand.

DROP & BAKE Drop the dough by rounded tablespoonfuls on ungreased baking sheets. Bake for 9 minutes, or until edges are light brown. Transfer to wire racks to cool.

Makes 4 dozen cookies

Per cookie: 130 calories, 1g protein, 17g carbohydrates, 6g fat, 2g saturated fat, 10mg cholesterol, 80mg sodium

Oodle-Kadoodles

SuperQuick

S'MORES

Prep **5 MINUTES**   *Microwave* **10 SECONDS**

2	graham crackers
1	bar (1.55 ounces) milk chocolate
2	large marshmallows

What could be better than an authentic recipe for S'mores, now cooked in seconds in the microwave!

LET'S BEGIN Break the graham crackers and chocolate in half. Center one section of chocolate on top of 2 graham cracker halves. Top each with a marshmallow.

MELT IT Place on a paper towel and microwave on High for 10 to 15 seconds until the marshmallow puffs.

STACK & SERVE Top each with another graham cracker half; press gently. Let stand for 1 minute to soften the chocolate. Serve immediately.

Makes 2 snacks

Per cookie: 222 calories, 3g protein, 35g carbohydrates, 8g fat, 4g saturated fat, 5mg cholesterol, 114mg sodium

Baking Basics

MORE S'MORES

These cookies come with many different flavors and fillings. Pick out one of these, then proceed as in original recipe.

PEANUT-Y S'MORES
Spread a thin layer of creamy or crunchy peanut butter on graham crackers.

CHOCOLATE-BANANA S'MORES
Place a slice of banana on top of the chocolate bar.

CHOCO-BERRY S'MORES
Place slices of strawberries on top of the chocolate bar.

RASPBERRY S'MORES
Spread a thin layer of seedless raspberry preserves on the graham crackers.

CHOCOLATE TEDDY BEARS

Prep **30 MINUTES**   *Microwave* **2 MINUTES**   *Chill* **30 MINUTES**

1   package (10 ounces) peanut butter chips (1⅔ cups)

1   cup semisweet chocolate chips

2   tablespoons shortening (do not use butter, margarine spread, or oil)

1   package (20 ounces) chocolate sandwich cookies

1   box (10 ounces) teddy bear-shaped graham snack crackers

Here, store-bought cookies are dipped into a melted peanut-chocolate mixture and topped with a graham-cracker teddy. How cute!

LET'S BEGIN Cover tray or cookie sheet with waxed paper.

COOK & STIR Place the peanut butter chips, chocolate chips, and shortening in a medium microwavable bowl. Microwave on High for 1½ to 2 minutes, or until the chips have melted and the mixture is smooth when stirred. Using a fork, dip each cookie into the chip mixture and tap the fork gently on the side of the bowl to remove the excess chocolate.

CHILL IT Put the coated cookies on the tray and top each cookie with a graham snack cracker. Refrigerate, uncovered, for 30 minutes, or until the chocolate is set.

Makes 4 dozen cookies

Per cookie: 138 calories, 2g protein, 18g carbohydrates, 6g fat, 3g saturated fat, 0mg cholesterol, 122mg sodium

PEANUT BLOSSOMS

Prep **30 MINUTES**   *Bake* **8 MINUTES**

1   bag (8 ounces) chocolate candy kisses

1½   cups all-purpose flour

1   teaspoon baking soda

½   teaspoon salt

½   cup shortening

¾   cup creamy or crunchy peanut butter

⅓   cup granulated sugar plus extra for coating

⅓   cup packed light brown sugar

1   large egg

2   tablespoons milk

1   teaspoon vanilla extract

Here are thumbprints with a twist. Chocolate kisses fill the centers of buttery, peanut-y cookies—all sparkling with sugar.

LET'S BEGIN Preheat the oven to 375°F. Remove the wrappers from the chocolates. Stir the flour, baking soda, and salt in a small bowl.

MIX IT UP Beat the shortening and peanut butter in a large bowl with an electric mixer on medium speed until well blended. Add both of the sugars and beat until fluffy. Beat in the egg, milk, and vanilla and blend in the flour mixture.

DROP & BAKE Shape dough into 1-inch balls and roll in granulated sugar. Place on ungreased cookie sheets. Bake for 8 to 10 minutes, until light brown. Quickly press a chocolate into the center of each (cookie will crack slightly). Transfer cookies to wire rack. Cool completely.

Makes 4 dozen cookies
Per cookie: 96 calories, 2g protein, 10g carbohydrates, 6g fat, 2g saturated fat, 6mg cholesterol, 75mg sodium

CHOCOLATE X'S & O'S

Prep **20 MINUTES**   *Chill* **30 MINUTES**   *Bake* **5 MINUTES**

2½   cups all-purpose flour

½   cup cocoa

½   teaspoon baking soda

¼   teaspoon salt

⅔   cup butter or margarine, softened

1   cup sugar

2   teaspoons vanilla extract

2   large eggs

2   tablespoons light corn syrup

Decorator's icing
(see page 133)

At that next birthday party, how about a "giant" game of tic-tac-toe? They make great sundae toppers, too.

LET'S BEGIN Preheat the oven to 350°F. For the flour mixture, combine the first four ingredients.

MIX IT IN Beat the butter, sugar, and vanilla in a large bowl with an electric mixer on medium speed until fluffy. Beat in the eggs, then the corn syrup. Gradually beat in flour mixture. Cover and refrigerate for 30 minutes, or until firm.

INTO THE OVEN Using rounded teaspoons of dough, shape two-thirds of dough into 3-inch logs and the remaining dough into 5-inch logs. To make X's, use two 3-inch logs to form X's. To make O's, use 5-inch logs to form circle-O's. Bake on ungreased cookie sheets for 5 minutes, or until set. Transfer from cookie sheet to wire rack to cool. Decorate with icing.

Makes 5 dozen cookies

Per cookie: 57 calories, 1g protein, 8g carbohydrates, 2g fat, 1g saturated fat, 13mg cholesterol, 46mg sodium

Nutty Mallow Grahamwiches

NUTTY MALLOW GRAHAMWICHES

Prep **20 MINUTES**   *Chill* **20 MINUTES**

¼   **cup butter or margarine**

¼   **cup creamy peanut butter**

1   **package (10½ ounces) miniature marshmallows**

1   **cup dry-roasted peanuts**

24   **squares chocolate graham crackers**

1   **package (8 squares) semisweet baking chocolate, chopped**

Here, graham crackers sandwich a heavenly filling of peanut butter, peanuts, and marshmallows. Plus, a dip of chocolate, too!

LET'S BEGIN Cook and stir the butter, peanut butter, and 3½ cups of the marshmallows in a large saucepan over medium-low heat for 6 minutes, or until marshmallows melt. Add the peanuts and remaining marshmallows; mix well.

OFF THE SPOON Quickly spoon ¼ cup of marshmallow mixture onto 12 grahams; top with remaining grahams.

CHILL IT Melt chocolate in a small saucepan over low heat, stirring constantly. Dip the sandwiches, diagonally, halfway into the chocolate. Place on waxed paper-lined cookie sheet. Refrigerate for 20 to 30 minutes, until chocolate is set.

Makes 1 dozen cookies
Per cookie: 370 calories, 7g protein, 42g carbohydrates, 22g fat, 9g saturated fat, 11mg cholesterol, 122mg sodium

S'MORE BARS

Prep **15 MINUTES**   *Bake* **25 MINUTES**

½   **cup margarine**

1½   **cups graham cracker crumbs**

1   **cup semisweet chocolate chips**

1   **cup butterscotch chips**

1   **cup miniature marshmallows**

1   **can (14 ounces) low-fat sweetened condensed milk**

Turn those campfire favorites of S'mores into heavenly cookie bars.

LET'S BEGIN Preheat oven to 350°F. Put margarine in microwavable cup. Cook on High for 1 minute, until melted. Pour into 13 × 9-inch baking dish and spread to coat.

INTO THE PAN Sprinkle graham cracker crumbs over bottom of dish to cover. Layer: chocolate chips, butterscotch chips, and marshmallows. Pour milk evenly over all.

INTO THE OVEN Bake for 25 minutes, or until bubbly. Let cool before cutting into squares.

Makes 2 dozen bars
Per bar: 197 calories, 2g protein, 28g carbohydrates, 9g fat, 5g saturated fat, 2mg cholesterol, 125mg sodium

CHOCOLATE CARAMEL & NUT TREATS

Prep **5 MINUTES**   *Cook* **8 MINUTES**

12	double (5 × 2½-inch) graham crackers
¾	cup firmly packed brown sugar
¾	cup butter
1	package (6 ounces) semisweet real chocolate chips (1 cup)
1	cup salted peanuts

When using brown sugar, be sure to press down firmly into the measuring cup to ensure that you get the proper amount. If the sugar turns hard in the box, microwave it for a couple of seconds.

LET'S BEGIN Line a 15 × 10-inch jelly-roll pan with graham crackers and set aside.

BUBBLE & BOIL Bring the sugar and butter to a full boil in a medium saucepan over medium heat. Boil 5 minutes, stirring constantly.

COAT & SPRINKLE Immediately pour the mixture over the graham crackers. Spread out evenly and sprinkle with the chocolate chips. Let stand for 1 minute to melt the chips, then spread out the chocolate. Sprinkle the peanuts on top and lightly press into the chocolate. Cool, then break into pieces.

Makes 4 dozen cookies

Per cookie: 100 calories, 1g protein, 11g carbohydrates, 6g fat, 3g saturated fat, 10mg cholesterol, 110mg sodium

JIMMY JUMBLES

Prep **15 MINUTES**   *Bake* **14 MINUTES**

2 cups all-purpose flour

1½ cups quick-cooking oats

1 teaspoon baking soda

½ teaspoon salt

1 cup granulated sugar

1 cup firmly packed brown sugar

1 cup butter, softened

2 large eggs

1 tablespoon vanilla extract

1 cup coarsely chopped salted peanuts

1 package (14 ounces) candy-coated milk chocolate pieces (2 cups)

Jumbles are moist and extra-large cookies. Watch them disappear from your cookie jar—one, two, three.

LET'S BEGIN Preheat the oven to 350°F. Grease 2 cookie sheets. For the flour mixture, combine the first four ingredients.

MIX IT IN Beat both of the sugars, butter, eggs, and vanilla in a large bowl with an electric mixer on medium speed for 2 to 3 minutes, until light and fluffy. Reduce the speed to low and blend in the flour mixture. Stir in the peanuts and candy.

DROP & BAKE Drop dough by ¼ cupfuls, 2 inches apart on cookie sheets. Bake for 14 minutes, or until light golden brown. Let stand 1 minute, then transfer to wire racks to cool.

Makes 2 dozen cookies

Per cookie: 320 calories, 5g protein, 42g carbohydrates, 15g fat, 8g saturated fat, 40mg cholesterol, 220mg sodium

CLASSIC CHOCOLATE CHIPS

Prep **25 MINUTES**   *Bake* **8 MINUTES**

2¼ cups all-purpose flour

1   teaspoon baking soda

½   teaspoon salt

1   cup butter, softened

¾   cup granulated sugar

¾   cup packed light brown sugar

1   teaspoon vanilla extract

2   large eggs

1   package semisweet chocolate chips (12 ounces)

1   cup chopped nuts (optional)

No one ever gets tired of these all-American favorites. Bake larger cookies, adding a few minutes more bake time. Put two cookies together with vanilla ice cream to make ice cream sandwiches.

LET'S BEGIN Preheat the oven to 375°F. Stir the flour, baking soda, and salt, in a small bowl.

MIX IT UP Beat the butter, both of the sugars, and vanilla together in a large bowl with an electric mixer on medium speed until creamy. Beat in the eggs, then the flour mixture. Stir in the chocolate chips and nuts, if you like. Drop by rounded teaspoons on ungreased cookie sheets.

INTO THE OVEN Bake for 8 to 10 minutes, until light brown. Cool slightly and transfer to wire rack.

Makes 4 dozen cookies

Per cookie: 120 calories, 1g protein, 15g carbohydrates, 6g fat, 4g saturated fat, 20mg cholesterol, 97mg sodium

PEANUT MARBLES

Prep **25 MINUTES**

1   cup confectioners' sugar

1   cup peanut butter

⅓   cup milk

1   teaspoon vanilla extract

1½   cups quick-cooking or
       old-fashioned oats

1   cup granola cereal

1¼   cups peanut butter and
       milk chocolate pieces

Your kids will never guess these pop-in-your-mouth morsels are made with healthy oats. They're chunky, chewy, and yummy.

LET'S BEGIN Combine the first four ingredients in a large bowl and mix well.

MIX IT UP Stir in the oats, granola, and candy pieces and mix until the cereal is completely coated.

BLEND IT IN Roll and press the cookie mixture into 1-inch balls and place on waxed paper–lined cookie sheets. Let stand until firm. Store between sheets of waxed paper in a tightly covered container in the refrigerator.

Makes 3 dozen cookies

Per cookie: 128 calories, 4g protein, 14 carbohydrates, 7g fat, 3g saturated fat, 1mg cholesterol, 125mg sodium

Chocolate Macadamia Cookies, page 95

Lots of Chocolate

Calling all chocolate lovers—here's a collection of chocolate cookies like none other. We've chosen the best of the best! Naturally there are brownies and lots of them—truffle brownies, deep chocolate brownies with white chips, and even brownies that have been dropped into cookies instead of baked into bars. Many are super-fast to fix since they need no baking at all. We've added tips on working with chocolate, such as the fastest way to melt chocolate chips—in the microwave, of course. Expect fabulous old-fashioned flavor in our cookies, too. Some are dipped in chocolate, others made with two or three kinds of chocolate, still others rolled in chocolate. Try one right now!

DIVINE TRUFFLE BROWNIES

Prep **15 MINUTES**   *Microwave* **3 MINUTES**   *Bake* **35 MINUTES**

1	package (8 ounces) semisweet baking chocolate (8 squares)
¼	cup butter or margarine
¾	cup sugar
3	large eggs
¾	cup all-purpose flour
⅔	cup heavy cream

We all love truffles for their wickedly rich chocolate taste and melt-in-the-mouth texture. These cookies are a perfect substitute. Since they're so rich, cut into 1-inch squares, if you wish.

LET'S BEGIN Preheat the oven to 350°F. Line an 8-inch square baking pan with foil, letting it extend over the edges of the pan. Butter the foil. Combine 2 squares of the chocolate and the butter in a medium microwavable bowl and microwave on High for 1½ minutes, or until the butter melts. Stir until the chocolate melts and the mixture is smooth.

MIX & BLEND Stir in ½ cup of the sugar, then 1 egg until well blended. Blend in the flour. Spread the batter evenly in the pan. Combine the remaining 6 squares of chocolate and the cream in a microwavable bowl and microwave on High for 1½ minutes; stir until the chocolate melts. Beat the remaining ¼ cup sugar and the remaining 2 eggs in a large bowl with an electric mixer on high speed until the mixture is thick and lemon colored. Beat in the chocolate-cream mixture until blended. Pour it over the batter in the pan.

INTO THE OVEN Bake for 35 minutes, or until the mousse topping has set (it will look firm on the top and barely shake in the center). Transfer the brownies in the pan to a wire rack to cool completely. Run a knife around the edges of the pan to loosen the brownies from the sides of the pan. Lift the brownies out of the pan using the foil extensions as handles. Cut into 2-inch squares.

Makes 16 brownies
Per brownie: 203 calories, 3g protein, 22g carbohydrates, 12g fat, 7g saturated fat, 62mg cholesterol, 47mg sodium

WHITE CHIP BROWNIES

Prep **15 MINUTES**   *Bake* **25 MINUTES**

1⅓   cups all-purpose flour

⅔   cup unsweetened cocoa

1   teaspoon baking powder

½   teaspoon salt

4   large eggs

1¼   cups sugar

½   cup butter or margarine, melted

2   teaspoons vanilla extract

1   package (10 ounces) white chips

Lots of rich cocoa powder and white chocolate chips make these one-bowl brownies special. To blend dry ingredients, whisk them together. This aerates and blends them, making lighter cookies.

LET'S BEGIN Preheat the oven to 350°F. Butter a 13 × 9-inch baking pan. For the flour mixture, combine the first four ingredients in a large bowl.

BLEND IT IN Beat the eggs in a large bowl with a wooden spoon until foamy. Gradually beat in the sugar, then beat in the butter and vanilla until well blended. Add the flour mixture to the egg mixture, mixing until blended. Gently stir in the white chips.

INTO THE OVEN Scrape the batter into the pan, spreading it evenly. Bake for 25 to 30 minutes, until the brownies begin to pull away from the sides of the pan. Transfer to a wire rack to cool completely. Cut into bars.

Makes 32 brownies

Per brownie: 133 calories, 2g protein, 18g carbohydrates, 6g fat, 4g saturated fat, 35mg cholesterol, 100mg sodium

CHOCOLATE TOFFEE BARS

Prep **25 MINUTES + CHILLING**   *Bake* **35 MINUTES**   *Microwave* **4 MINUTES**

1   cup butter or margarine, softened

1   cup packed brown sugar

1   large egg yolk

1½   cups all-purpose flour

¼   teaspoon salt

½   cup light corn syrup

¼   cup heavy cream

1   teaspoon vanilla extract

1   package (8 ounces) semisweet baking chocolate, chopped

1   cup chopped pecans, toasted

Think of these amazing sweets as one gigantic toffee bar.

LET'S BEGIN Preheat the oven to 350°F. Line a 13 × 9-inch baking pan with foil and lightly butter the foil.

MIX IT IN Cream ¾ cup each of the butter and brown sugar in a large bowl with an electric mixer on medium speed until light. Beat in egg yolk. Reduce the speed to low and blend in the flour and salt. Press the dough into the pan. Bake for 16 to 18 minutes, until golden brown. Cool on wire rack.

COOK & STIR Combine the remaining ¼ cup butter, the remaining ¼ cup brown sugar, the corn syrup, heavy cream, and vanilla in a large microwavable bowl. Microwave on High for 4 minutes, stirring after 2 minutes. Spread the mixture evenly over the crust. Bake for 18 to 20 minutes, until set. Sprinkle with the chopped chocolate. Bake for 1 to 2 minutes, until the chocolate melts. Spread the chocolate evenly with a narrow metal spatula, then sprinkle with the pecans. Cool completely on wire rack. Refrigerate for 30 minutes, or until the chocolate is firm. Cut into bars or diamonds.

Makes 3 dozen bars

Per bar: 162 calories, 1g protein, 17g carbohydrates, 10g fat, 5g saturated fat, 23mg cholesterol, 80mg sodium

Cook to Cook

HOW CAN I KEEP CHOCOLATE SMOOTH WHEN MELTING IT?

"I've found that even a droplet or two of water or other liquid will turn chocolate grainy during melting. So I always make sure that *all utensils I use are completely dry.* Don't worry if you're using a lot of liquid though, as it will not cause the chocolate to clump or turn grainy. It's all a matter of proportion. Remove chocolate as soon as it's melted. Avoid overheating!

If chocolate turns grainy, make it smooth again by adding a teaspoon of solid shortening for each one-ounce square of chocolate (no margarine or butter, please, for they may cloud it)."

CHOCOLATE-COCONUT PECAN SQUARES

Prep **25 MINUTES**   *Bake* **38 MINUTES**

¾ cup margarine or butter

¾ cup sugar

1¼ cups all-purpose flour

2 tablespoons heavy cream

1¾ cups pecans, coarsely chopped

1 cup flaked sweetened coconut

4 squares (4 ounces) semisweet baking chocolate, coarsely chopped

Pecans are perfect in these cookies, but you can substitute walnuts or almonds. The cookies will still taste great, but not quite as rich.

LET'S BEGIN Preheat the oven to 350°F. Cream ½ cup of the margarine and ¼ cup of the sugar in a large bowl with an electric mixer on medium speed until light and fluffy. Reduce the speed to low and blend in the flour until a dough forms. Press into an ungreased 9-inch square baking pan. Bake for 18 to 20 minutes, until the edges are light brown.

COOK & STIR Combine the remaining ½ cup sugar, the remaining ¼ cup margarine, and the heavy cream in a small saucepan and cook, stirring, over medium-low heat, until the margarine melts and the mixture is smooth. Stir in the pecans.

INTO THE OVEN Sprinkle the coconut and chocolate evenly over the crust. Top with the pecan mixture, spreading it evenly. Bake for 20 to 25 minutes, until golden. Transfer the bars in the pan to a wire rack to cool completely. Cut into squares.

Makes 16 squares

Per square: 304 calories, 3g protein, 25g carbohydrates, 23g fat, 7g saturated fat, 3mg cholesterol, 123mg sodium

Baking Basics

2 QUICK WAYS TO KEEP COOKIES EXTRA FRESH!

The crispest cookies can turn soft and soggy if not stored properly. To keep crisp cookies crisp and chewy cookies chewy, store them separately in different cookie jars—never together. If stored together, crisp cookies might soften and soft cookies might harden.

To Crisp Up Crisp Cookies—If you like your cookies crisp and they have softened after standing, spread them out on a cookie sheet and place them in a 300°F oven for 3 to 5 minutes. Transfer them to wire racks and let them cool completely before storing.

To Keep Soft Cookies Soft—Store them in a cookie jar or container with a tight-fitting lid. Add a piece of bread to the container, changing it every day to keep cookies soft. This technique also works with soft cookies that have become dry and hardened.

LAYERED CHOCOLATE-PEANUT BUTTER BARS

Prep **25 MINUTES**   *Bake* **25 MINUTES**

1½   cups smooth peanut butter

½   cup butter or margarine, softened

1   cup sugar

3   large eggs

1   cup all-purpose flour

1   package (8 ounces) semisweet baking chocolate, melted (8 squares)

1   cup chopped salted peanuts

You might think that unsalted peanuts would be better in a cookie recipe, but don't substitute. The salt complements the chocolate, bringing out the chocolate taste and making it sensational.

LET'S BEGIN Preheat the oven to 350°F. Line a 13 × 9-inch baking pan with foil, extending the foil over the edges of the pan. Beat the peanut butter and butter in a large bowl with an electric mixer on medium speed until light. Add the sugar and eggs and beat until well blended. Reduce the speed to low and blend in the flour until mixed well. Remove 1½ cups of this peanut butter mixture and set aside.

PRESS & TOP Add one-half of the melted chocolate to the remaining peanut butter mixture; beat until well blended. Press into the prepared pan. Spread the reserved peanut butter mixture evenly over the top.

INTO THE OVEN Bake for 25 minutes, or until the edges are light brown. Spread the remaining melted chocolate evenly over the top. Sprinkle with the peanuts. Transfer the bars to a wire rack to cool completely. Lift the bars out of the pan using the foil extensions as handles. Cut into pieces.

Makes 3 dozen bars

Per bar: 181 calories, 5g protein, 14g carbohydrates, 13g fat, 4g saturated fat, 25mg cholesterol, 100mg sodium

CHOCOLATE RASPBERRY SQUARES

Prep **25 MINUTES**   *Bake* **25 MINUTES**

1¼   cups all-purpose flour

1¼   cups oats (quick-cooking or old-fashioned)

⅓   cup granulated sugar

⅓   cup packed brown sugar

½   teaspoon baking powder

¼   teaspoon salt

¾   cup cold margarine or butter, cut into pieces

¾   cup raspberry jam

1   package (6 ounces) semisweet chocolate chips

Royal Icing (see page 133, optional)

You can use quick or old-fashioned oats interchangeably. The only difference is that quick oats are cut into smaller pieces so they cook faster. Nutritionally, they mirror each other.

LET'S BEGIN Preheat the oven to 375°F. Combine the flour, oats, granulated and brown sugars, baking powder, and salt in a large bowl. Cut in the margarine with a pastry cutter or 2 knives used scissor-fashion until the mixture is crumbly. Reserve 1 cup of the oat mixture.

INTO THE OVEN Press the remaining oat mixture into an ungreased 8-inch square baking pan. Bake for 10 minutes.

TOP & BAKE Spread the jam evenly over the partially baked crust, leaving a ¼-inch border all around. Top with chocolate chips. Sprinkle the reserved oat mixture over the chocolate chips, patting it gently. Bake for 30 to 35 minutes, until the topping is golden brown. Transfer to a wire rack to cool. Swirl with white icing if you wish. Cut into squares.

Makes 3 dozen squares

Per square: 115 calories, 1g protein, 17g carbohydrates, 5g fat, 2g saturated fat, 0mg cholesterol, 70mg sodium

Time Savers

2 QUICK WAYS TO DRIZZLE GLAZE

Use the Royal Icing recipe (page 133), adding a little extra liquid to make it thin enough to drizzle. Dip the prongs of a fork or the tip of a spoon into the glaze and drizzle all over in any design you choose.

Pour the glaze into a small self-closing plastic bag. Cut off a small diagonal piece from one corner. Then, pipe the glaze onto the cookies in a swirl or zigzag design. Perfect for bars cookies!

DOUBLY CHOCOLATE COOKIES

Prep **20 MINUTES**   *Bake* **8 MINUTES**

2	cups all-purpose flour
²/₃	cup unsweetened cocoa
¾	teaspoon baking soda
¼	teaspoon salt
1	cup butter or margarine, softened
1½	cups sugar
2	large eggs
2	teaspoons vanilla
1	package (12 ounces) semisweet chocolate chips
½	cup coarsely chopped nuts (optional)

There is a reason why some recipes tell you to let cookies cool before moving them. They're fragile when hot, then firm up. Let these cookies cool on the cookie sheet about 5 minutes.

LET'S BEGIN Preheat the oven to 350°F. Combine the flour, cocoa, baking soda, and salt in a medium bowl.

BLEND IT IN Cream the butter, sugar, eggs, and vanilla in a large bowl with an electric mixer on medium speed until light and fluffy. Reduce the speed to low and gradually blend in the flour mixture. Stir in the chips and nuts, if you like.

DROP & BAKE Drop the dough by rounded teaspoonfuls on ungreased cookie sheets. Bake for 8 to 10 minutes, just until set. Cool slightly, then transfer to wire racks to cool completely.

Makes about 4¹/₂ dozen cookies

Per cookie: 105 calories, 1g protein, 13g carbohydrates, 6g fat, 4g saturated fat, 18mg cholesterol, 68mg sodium

CHOCOLATE MACADAMIA COOKIES

Prep **20 MINUTES**   *Bake* **8 MINUTES**

1	package (18½ ounces) chocolate chip–cookie mix
½	cup unsweetened cocoa
⅓	cup vegetable oil
1	large egg
2	tablespoons water
⅔	cup macadamia nuts, coarsely chopped

Macadamia nuts are very delicious and very rich. They are higher in fat than most other nuts, so you don't need to use as many.

LET'S BEGIN Preheat the oven to 375°F.

MIX IT UP Combine the cookie mix and cocoa in a bowl. Stir in the oil, egg, and water until blended. Stir in the nuts.

DROP & BAKE Drop the dough by rounded teaspoonfuls 2 inches apart on ungreased cookie sheets. Bake for 8 to 10 minutes, until set. Cool slightly, then transfer to wire racks.

Makes about 3 dozen cookies

Per cookie: 99 calories, 1g protein, 5g carbohydrates, 2g fat, 1g saturated fat, 6mg cholesterol, 27mg sodium

NO-BAKE CHOCOLATE COOKIES

Prep **20 MINUTES + CHILLING**   *Microwave* **1 MINUTE**

1	package (6 ounces) semisweet chocolate chips
1	cup butterscotch pieces
1½	cups oats (quick-cooking or old-fashioned)
1	cup salted chopped peanuts

Four ingredients never tasted so good! And these cookies are whipped up in the microwave. What could be easier?

LET'S BEGIN Line a large cookie sheet with waxed paper.

COOK & STIR Combine the chocolate and butterscotch chips in a microwavable bowl. Microwave on High for 30 seconds to 1½ minutes, until the mixture melts and is smooth, stirring every 30 seconds. Add the oats and peanuts and mix well.

CHILL IT Drop the dough by heaping teaspoonfuls on the cookie sheet. Chill for 30 minutes, or until firm. Store in a tightly covered container in the refrigerator.

Makes 3 dozen cookies

Per cookie: 85 calories, 2g protein, 9g carbohydrates, 5g fat, 2g saturated fat, 0mg cholesterol, 23mg sodium

CHOCOLATE BROWNIE COOKIES

Prep **25 MINUTES**   *Bake* **12 MINUTES**

3	large eggs
1	cup turbinado sugar
1	tablespoon brewed espresso or strong brewed coffee
1	teaspoon vanilla extract
6	tablespoons all-purpose flour
½	teaspoon baking powder
¼	teaspoon salt
6	ounces bittersweet chocolate
3	squares (3 ounces) unsweetened baking chocolate
1½	tablespoons butter
1	cup mini semisweet chocolate chips

What could be more fabulous than a cookie that tastes like a brownie? This one has three kinds of chocolate: semisweet chips and bittersweet and unsweetened chocolate. Wow!

LET'S BEGIN Preheat the oven to 325°F. Mix the eggs, sugar, espresso, and vanilla in a small bowl. Combine the flour, baking powder, and salt in a medium bowl.

MIX IT IN Melt the bittersweet and unsweetened chocolates and butter in a medium saucepan over low heat, stirring until smooth. Gently fold in the egg mixture, then fold in the flour mixture. Fold in the chocolate chips. Do not overmix the batter.

INTO THE OVEN Drop teaspoonfuls of the batter on an ungreased cookie sheet. Bake for 12 minutes, or until the cookies puff and form cracks. Transfer to wire racks to cool completely.

Makes 2 dozen cookies
Per cookie: 108 calories, 2g protein, 10g carbohydrates, 8g fat, 3g saturated fat, 17mg cholesterol, 40mg sodium

---

Food Facts

HOW TO CHOOSE THE RIGHT CHOCOLATE FOR YOUR RECIPE!

Cookies just wouldn't be the same without chocolate—but you must use the right one! Here's how they differ. Be sure to follow your recipe when choosing them.

Unsweetened chocolate: This chocolate has no sugar at all, only cocoa solids (chocolate liquor) and cocoa butter. It's the perfect, usually inexpensive chocolate to use in brownies, but don't forget the sugar!

Bittersweet & semisweet chocolate: Both forms of this chocolate are sweetened with a minimum of 35 percent of chocolate liquor or chocolate solids. Bittersweet chocolate has the least amount of sugar and is the perfect one to add to cookie doughs. Melt it or chop into fine chips or chunks.

German chocolate: This chocolate is both sweet and dark chocolate—perfect to melt for cookie doughs.

CHOCOLATE-DIPPED CRANBERRY COOKIES

Prep **30 MINUTES + COOLING**   *Bake* **10 MINUTES**

2	cups all-purpose flour
1	teaspoon baking powder
½	teaspoon salt
1	cup vegetable shortening
1	cup sugar
1	large egg
1	teaspoon vanilla extract
2	cups fresh or frozen cranberries, coarsely chopped
1⅓	cups semisweet chocolate chips, melted
1¼	cups chopped nuts

When dipping the cookies into the melted chocolate, let the excess drip off, then wipe the bottoms of the cookies on the rim of the bowl to remove extra chocolate.

LET'S BEGIN Preheat the oven to 350°F. Combine the flour, baking powder, and salt in a large bowl.

BLEND IT IN Cream the shortening and sugar in a medium bowl with an electric mixer on medium speed until light and fluffy. Beat in the egg and vanilla until mixed well. Reduce the speed to low and blend in the flour mixture, mixing until a soft dough forms. Stir in the cranberries.

DROP & BAKE Drop the dough by rounded teaspoonfuls on buttered cookie sheets. Bake for 10 minutes, or until golden brown. Transfer the cookies to wire racks to cool completely. Dip each cookie halfway into the melted chocolate and then into the nuts. Place the cookies on a sheet of waxed paper and set aside until the chocolate sets.

Makes about 3 dozen cookies

Per cookie: 155 calories, 2g protein, 16g carbohydrates, 10g fat, 3g saturated fat, 8mg cholesterol, 48mg sodium

Microwave in Minutes

THE FASTEST WAY TO MELT CHOCOLATE CHIPS

Use your microwave to melt chocolate chips. It's not only fast but also easy. Put 1 cup (6 ounces) of chocolate chips (regular-size morsels) in a microwavable bowl. Microwave on High for 1 minute, then stir. Continue to cook in 10-second intervals, stirring, until chips melt, lose their shape, and become smooth. Watch carefully and do not overcook! To melt 2 cups of chips, microwave a few more seconds, until smooth.

PISTACHIO-WHITE CHOCOLATE CHIP COOKIES

Prep **25 MINUTES**   *Bake* **9 MINUTES**

It's always a good idea to stir in dry ingredients, as well as candy chips and nuts, by hand to avoid toughening the dough.

½	cup butter, softened
1	cup packed brown sugar
½	cup granulated sugar
½	cup vegetable shortening
2	large eggs
1	tablespoon vanilla extract
3	cups all-purpose flour
1	teaspoon baking soda
½	teaspoon salt
1½	cups shelled pistachios
1	package (12 ounces) white baking chips

LET'S BEGIN Preheat the oven to 375°F.

MIX IT IN Cream the butter, brown sugar, granulated sugar, and shortening in a large bowl with an electric mixer on medium speed until light and fluffy. Add the eggs and vanilla, beating until well mixed. Reduce the speed to low and blend in the flour, baking soda, and salt until well mixed. Stir in the pistachios and white baking chips by hand.

DROP & BAKE Drop the dough by rounded tablespoonfuls about 2 inches apart on ungreased cookie sheets. Bake for 9 to 11 minutes, until light brown. Transfer the cookies to wire racks to cool completely.

Makes 3½ dozen cookies
Per cookie: 180 calories, 3g protein, 20g carbohydrates, 9g fat, 4g saturated fat, 6mg cholesterol, 130mg sodium

---

Cook to Cook

HOW CAN I SHIP COOKIES SO THEY DON'T CRUMBLE?

❝*Some cookies just ship better than others,* so I always choose my recipe very carefully. Soft drop cookies, such as chocolate chip cookies, and chunky-chewy cookies, such as oatmeal raisin cookies, are great to ship. Bar cookies such as brownies and nut bars ship well, too. Avoid cookies that are brittle or fragile, such as thin sugar cookies.

Wrapping the cookies carefully is very important! If you're shipping bar cookies, it's best to wrap them first in plastic wrap. Be sure to wrap the same types and flavors together. To save time, I wrap two cookies together, back to back. Pack them in a sturdy cardboard box or tin.

Line it with bubble wrap, leaving an overhang. Tuck in the cookies and enclose them in the wrap. If they're fragile, I often put this box into another one before mailing. To be sure they arrive fresh, I usually splurge and send in overnight priority mail.❞

APRICOT & CRANBERRY WHITE CHOCOLATE CHUNKS

Prep **25 MINUTES**   *Bake* **11 MINUTES**

1¾   cups all-purpose flour

1   teaspoon salt

¾   teaspoon baking soda

¾   cup unsalted butter, margarine, or butter-flavored shortening

1¼   cups packed light brown sugar

1   large egg

2   tablespoons milk

1   teaspoon vanilla extract

1   teaspoon coconut extract

1   cup white chocolate chunks

¾   cup chopped dried apricots

½   cup dried cranberries

½   cup chopped macadamia nuts

Here's a cookie that's perfect for the holidays, and any special day. It's chock full of fruit, nuts, and heavenly bits of white chocolate.

LET'S BEGIN Preheat the oven to 375°F. Combine the flour, salt, and baking soda in a medium bowl.

MIX IT UP Cream the butter and brown sugar in a large bowl with an electric mixer on medium speed until light and fluffy. Beat in the egg, milk, vanilla, and coconut extract. Reduce the speed to low and blend in the flour mixture until well blended. Stir in the chocolate chunks, apricots, cranberries, and nuts.

DROP & BAKE Drop tablespoonfuls of the dough about 2 inches apart on ungreased cookie sheets. Bake the cookies for 11 to 13 minutes, until light brown. Cool for 1 minute on the sheets, then transfer to wire racks to cool completely.

Makes about 3 dozen cookies

Per cookie: 148 calories, 1g protein, 20g carbohydrates, 7g fat, 4g saturated fat, 17mg cholesterol, 108mg sodium

---

Food Facts

WHITE CHOCOLATE REALLY ISN'T CHOCOLATE AFTER ALL!

Because white chocolate contains cocoa butter—but no chocolate liquor or solids—it isn't technically considered real chocolate, even though it tastes somewhat like chocolate and performs a lot like it in recipes. White chocolate has a very low melting point, so it is rather sensitive to heat. It's usually melted and mixed into cookie dough for flavoring, or stirred into dough as chunks and chips.

CHOCOLATE-DIPPED HEARTS

Prep **40 MINUTES + CHILLING**   *Bake* **7 MINUTES**

DOUGH

1   cup butter, softened

1   package (3 ounces)
      cream cheese, softened

¾   cup sugar

1   large egg

1   teaspoon peppermint
      extract

3   cups all-purpose flour

GLAZE

1   package (12 ounces)
      semisweet chocolate
      chips

2   tablespoons vegetable
      shortening

Here's the perfect way to say "I love you!" Try substituting white chocolate or milk chocolate for the semisweet.

LET'S BEGIN Beat all of the dough ingredients except flour in a large bowl with an electric mixer on medium speed until creamy. Reduce speed to low and blend in flour. Divide dough in half, shape each piece into a disk, and wrap in plastic. Refrigerate at least 2 hours, until firm.

INTO THE OVEN Preheat oven to 375°F. Roll one piece of dough out on a lightly floured surface to a ¼-inch thickness. Cut out cookies with a 2½-inch heart-shaped cutter. Place 1 inch apart on ungreased cookie sheets. Repeat with the remaining dough. Bake for 7 to 10 minutes, until the edges are light brown. Transfer to wire racks to cool.

DECORATE Melt chocolate and shortening in a small saucepan over low heat. Dip half of each heart into chocolate. Place on waxed paper-lined cookie sheets. Chill until firm.

Makes 3½ dozen cookies
Per cookie: 140 calories, 2g protein, 16g carbohydrates, 8g fat, 5g saturated fat, 20mg cholesterol, 55mg sodium

---

Baking Basics

2 EASY STEPS FOR MELTING CHOCOLATE FOR DECORATING

When melting chocolate to dip cookies in, use this technique. It helps the chocolate to form a shiny, crisp coating. This also works when dipping fresh fruit and when making chocolate bark decorations.

1. **Chop bittersweet or semisweet chocolate** into small pieces and put them in a double boiler over simmering (not hot!) water. Be very careful to not get even one drop of water into the chocolate.

2. **Stir constantly** until two-thirds of the chocolate has melted. Remove from the heat, stirring until chocolate is smooth. While dipping, keep chocolate lukewarm over a bowl of warm water.

Mexican Chocolate Wedding Cakes

MEXICAN CHOCOLATE WEDDING CAKES

Prep **30 MINUTES**   *Bake* **8 MINUTES**   *Cool* **5 MINUTES**

¾	cup butter, softened
¾	cup packed brown sugar
3	ounces unsweetened baking chocolate, melted
1	teaspoon vanilla extract
2	cups all-purpose flour
½	teaspoon salt
1	cup finely chopped nuts

Confectioners' sugar

This is a sensational variation on the well-known vanilla-flavored, buttery wedding-cake cookies that just seem to melt in the mouth.

LET'S BEGIN Preheat the oven to 350°F. Cream the butter and brown sugar in a bowl with an electric mixer on medium speed until light. Beat in the melted chocolate and vanilla. Reduce the speed to low and add the flour, salt, and nuts, blending until well mixed.

DROP & BAKE Roll the dough into 1-inch balls. Place 2 inches apart on ungreased cookie sheets. Bake for 8 to 10 minutes, until set. Let rest for 5 minutes. Transfer to racks and cool for 5 minutes. Roll in confectioners' sugar while warm. When cookies are cool, roll again in the confectioners' sugar.

> *Makes 5 dozen cookies*
>
> *Per cookie: 70 calories, 1g protein, 8g carbohydrates, 4g fat, 2g saturated fat, 5mg cholesterol, 40mg sodium*

SuperQuick
CHOCOLATE TRUFFLE SNOWBALLS

Prep **25 MINUTES**   *Cook* **5 MINUTES**

8	ounces unsweetened chocolate, broken into pieces
½	cup + 1 to 2 tablespoons milk
1	package (1 pound) confectioners' sugar
1	cup chopped nuts

If you want these gems to resemble real truffles, when you roll them into balls don't make them perfectly round. Isn't that easy?

LET'S BEGIN Melt the chocolate with the ½ cup of the milk in a medium saucepan over low heat. Stir until smooth.

MIX & ROLL Set aside ½ cup of the confectioners' sugar. Blend in the remaining sugar into the chocolate mixture. Stir in the nuts. If the mixture seems dry, stir in the remaining milk 1 tablespoon at a time. Roll into 1-inch balls and dust with the reserved confectioners' sugar.

> *Makes about 5½ dozen cookies*
>
> *Per cookie: 57 calories, 1g protein, 8g carbohydrates, 3g fat, 1g saturated fat, 0mg cholesterol, 1mg sodium*

CHOCOLATE PUDDING COOKIES

Prep **25 MINUTES**   *Bake* **5 MINUTES**

Rich and chocolatey pudding mix makes these cookies extra-special—and extra easy to put together!

1	package (4-serving size) chocolate-flavor instant pudding & pie filling
1	cup all-purpose baking mix
¼	cup vegetable oil
1	large egg

Granulated sugar for sprinkling

LET'S BEGIN Preheat the oven to 350°F.

INTO THE BOWL Combine the pudding mix and baking mix in a large bowl. Stir in the oil and egg with a wooden spoon until the mixture forms a ball.

DROP & BAKE Roll the dough into ½-inch balls and place on ungreased cookie sheets. Flatten the balls with the bottom of a glass and sprinkle with sugar. Bake for 5 to 8 minutes, until slightly firm. Transfer to wire racks to cool.

Makes 3 dozen cookies

Per cookie: 42 calories, 0g protein, 5g carbohydrates, 2g fat, 0g saturated fat, 6mg cholesterol, 83mg sodium

Chocolate Pinwheels, page 111

Slice & Bake

Freshly baked cookies, right out of the oven—in minutes. So good and so simple, when you have a log of some slice 'n' bake cookie dough on hand. Here are those buttery, crispy icebox cookies of yesteryear with the popular chocolate swirls. But don't stop here. Our refrigerator cookies come with many new twists. Some are flavored with peanut butter and dipped into chocolate, others are freshened with lemon zest, and others come with a rich browned-butter flavor and a creamy vanilla filling. All take just minutes to mix, then walk away while the dough chills. Keep a log of these cookies in your refrigerator or freezer, and you can bake them at a moment's notice. Hot cookies anyone?

BROWNED-BUTTER CREAM SANDWICH COOKIES

Prep **30 MINUTES + CHILLING**   *Bake* **7 MINUTES**

1   cup butter, softened

⅔   cup packed brown sugar

2   large egg yolks

½   teaspoon vanilla extract

2½   cups all-purpose flour

⅓   cup finely chopped
         pecans

¼   teaspoon salt

**Browned-Butter Cream
Filling (see recipe)**

When butter is cooked until it turns hazelnut brown, it's called browned butter. It gives these cookies a rich nutty flavor.

LET'S BEGIN To make the cookies, cream the butter and the brown sugar in a large bowl with an electric mixer on medium speed until light and fluffy. Beat in the egg yolks and vanilla. Reduce the speed to low and blend in the flour, pecans, and salt until a ball of dough forms.

CHILL IT Divide the dough in half and shape each half into a 10-inch-long log (about 1½ inches in diameter). Wrap each roll tightly in plastic. Refrigerate 3 hours or overnight.

SLICE & BAKE Preheat the oven to 350°F. Cut logs with a sharp knife into ⅛-inch-thick slices. Place 2 inches apart on ungreased cookie sheets. Bake for 7 to 9 minutes, until the edges are light brown. Let stand for 1 minute, then transfer to wire racks to cool completely. While cookies cool, make the filling. Then, spread 1 level teaspoonful of the filling on the flat side of 1 cookie. Top with a second cookie, flat side down. Squeeze together gently. Repeat with the remaining cookies.

BROWNED-BUTTER CREAM FILLING

Melt and stir ¼ cup butter in a small saucepan over medium heat for 5 to 6 minutes or until butter just starts to brown. Butter with bubble and foam, so watch closely! Remove the pan immediately from the heat and cool for 5 minutes. Stir in 2 cups confectioners' sugar, ½ teaspoon vanilla extract, and about 2 to 3 tablespoons half-and-half, or enough to reach the desired spreading consistency. Use to fill sandwich cookies.

Makes 3½ dozen cookies
Per cookie: 120 calories, 1g protein, 15g carbohydrates, 7g fat, 4g saturated fat, 25mg cholesterol, 70mg sodium

CHOCOLATE PINWHEELS

Prep **30 MINUTES + CHILLING**   *Bake* **7 MINUTES**

1⅔   cups all-purpose flour

½   teaspoon baking powder

¼   teaspoon salt

½   cup butter, softened

1   cup sugar

1   large egg

2   teaspoons vanilla
    extract

2   squares (2 ounces)
    white baking bars,
    melted and cooled

1   square (1 ounce)
    unsweetened baking
    chocolate, melted and
    cooled

Pinwheel cookies are always fun to eat. Some like to eat them color by color, whereas others like to take a big bite to mix the flavors together. Either way, theses cookies taste great!

LET'S BEGIN For the flour mixture, combine the first three ingredients in a medium bowl. Beat the butter, sugar, egg, and vanilla in a large bowl with an electric mixer on medium speed until creamy. Reduce the speed to low and add the cooled melted white baking bars. Continue beating until well mixed. Blend in the flour mixture.

CHILL IT Remove half of the dough. Add the cooled melted chocolate to the remaining dough in bowl. Beat until well mixed. Shape each piece of dough into a 6 × 3-inch rectangle. Wrap in plastic and refrigerate for at least 1 hour, or until firm.

ROLL & CUT Preheat the oven to 375°F. Roll out the white dough on lightly floured waxed paper to a 15 × 7-inch rectangle. Repeat with chocolate dough. Place the chocolate dough on top of the white dough. Roll up jelly-roll style, starting with 15-inch side. (For easier handling, the roll can be cut in half.) Wrap the roll in plastic and refrigerate for at least 2 hours, or until firm. Cut the rolls into ¼-inch-thick slices and place 2 inches apart on ungreased cookie sheets. Bake for 7 to 9 minutes, until the edges begin to brown. Transfer to racks to cool completely.

Makes 5 dozen cookies

Per cookie: 50 calories, 1g protein, 7g carbohydrates, 3g fat, 1g saturated fat, 5mg cholesterol, 30mg sodium

MELT-IN-YOUR-MOUTH SHORTBREAD

Prep **30 MINUTES**   *Chill:* **2 HOURS**   *Bake* **7 MINUTES**

1   **cup butter, softened**

½   **cup firmly packed brown sugar**

1   **teaspoon vanilla extract**

2¼   **cups all-purpose flour**

½   **cup sugar**

1   **teaspoon ground cinnamon**

Bake up a batch of these buttery bites, brew up a pot of tea, and pretend you're in Scotland overlooking fields of blooming heather. It's as good as it gets!

LET'S BEGIN Cream the butter, brown sugar, and vanilla in a large bowl with an electric mixer on medium speed until light and creamy. Reduce the speed to low. Blend in the flour, scraping the bowl, until smooth.

SHAPE & CHILL Divide the dough in half and shape each into a 6 × 2-inch log. Wrap each log in plastic wrap and refrigerate for at least 2 hours.

INTO THE OVEN Preheat the oven to 375°F. Grease two cookie sheets. Slice dough into ¼-inch-thick slices and place 1-inch apart on the sheets. Bake for 7 to 9 minutes, until the edges are light brown. Let cookies rest on sheets for 5 minutes, then transfer to racks to cool. Mix the sugar and cinnamon in a bowl and roll the warm cookies in it to coat.

Makes 4 dozen cookies
Per cookie: 75 calories, 1g protein, 9g carbohydrates, 4g fat, 3g saturated fat, 11mg cholesterol, 42mg sodium

MARBLED SHORTBREADS

Melt 2 (1-ounce) squares semisweet baking chocolate or ⅓ cup semisweet real chocolate chips in 1-quart saucepan over low heat; cool 5 minutes. Meanwhile, prepare dough as directed above. Remove half of dough. Beat the cooled, melted chocolate into the remaining dough just until mixed. Shape four 6-inch logs: two plain and two chocolate. Press, mold, and shape one plain and one chocolate log together, creating a marbled 6-inch log. Repeat with remaining two pieces of dough. Wrap each log in plastic wrap; refrigerate until firm (at least 2 hours). Slice and bake as directed above. Roll warm cookies in ½ cup sugar (omit cinnamon).

CHOCOLATE-DIPPED REFRIGERATOR COOKIES

Prep **15 MINUTES + CHILLING**   *Bake* **8 MINUTES**

2½   cups all-purpose flour

1½   cups confectioners'
        sugar

2   teaspoons baking
        powder

½   teaspoon salt

1   cup unsalted butter or
        margarine, softened

1   large egg

1   teaspoon vanilla extract

1   cup semisweet chocolate
        chips, melted (6 ounces)

It is always quick to use a bag of premeasured chocolate chips—no weighing or measuring required. But, if you like, you can chop up enough bulk chocolate to equal 1 cup.

LET'S BEGIN Stir the flour, sugar, baking powder, and salt together in a medium bowl. Blend in the butter, egg, and vanilla. Divide into two equal parts and shape each into a 2-inch square log, about 8 inches long. Wrap each log tightly in plastic and refrigerate until well chilled, about 2 hours.

SLICE & BAKE Preheat the oven to 375°F. Butter cookie sheets or line with parchment paper. Using a sharp knife, cut the logs into ¼-inch-thick slices. Bake until edges are golden brown, about 8 minutes. Transfer to racks and cool completely.

DECORATE Dip the end of each cookie into the melted chocolate and cool until set.

Makes about 5 dozen cookies

Per cookie: 73 calories, 1g protein, 8g carbohydrates, 4g fat, 3g saturated fat, 12mg cholesterol, 37mg sodium

---

Baking Basics

3 SHAPES FROM ONE COOKIE

The shape of a refrigerator cookie is all in the log. Roll the log round into a cylinder shape, and your cookies will turn out in circles, like thin coins. Or, shape the log into one with straight sides, 1½ inches in diameter. Slice this log, and your cookies turn into squares. Slice each square diagonally, and you'll have triangular cookies to bake.

After baking, you can dip them in melted chocolate chips and coat with crushed peanuts for another flavor surprise. However you slice or dip them, slice & bakes are great!

SPICED ICEBOX COOKIES

Prep **10 MINUTES + CHILLING**   *Bake* **8 MINUTES**

2¼   cups sifted all-purpose
     flour

½   teaspoon baking soda

½   teaspoon ground
     cinnamon

½   teaspoon ground nutmeg

¼   teaspoon salt

½   cup butter, softened

1   cup packed dark brown
     sugar

1   large egg

1   teaspoon vanilla extract

1   cup pecans, finely
     chopped

Here's the most classic refrigerator cookie of them all. In fact, this recipes similar to the ones that were used before refrigerators became popular. They were known as icebox cookies in those days.

LET'S BEGIN For the flour mixture, combine the first five ingredients. Cream the butter and sugar in a large bowl with an electric mixer on medium speed until light and fluffy. Beat in the egg and vanilla. Reduce the speed to low and blend in the flour mixture, then stir in the pecans.

CHILL IT Shape the dough into two logs (about 1½ inches in diameter). Wrap the logs in plastic and refrigerate for at least 2 hours or overnight.

SLICE & BAKE Preheat the oven to 350°F. Butter 2 cookie sheets. Slice dough into ⅛-inch-thick slices and place on the cookie sheets. Bake for 8 to 10 minutes or just until edges start to brown. Transfer to wire racks to cool completely.

Makes about 7 dozen cookies

Per serving: 148 calories, 2g protein, 17g carbohydrates, 8g fat, 3g saturated fat, 22mg cholesterol, 96mg sodium

---

Cook to Cook

HOW DO YOU MAKE SANDWICH COOKIES?

❝ Whenever I have *refrigerator sugar cookie dough on-hand, I love to make sandwich cookies.* Just slice the dough ⅛-inch thick and bake them as usual. If I'm in a hurry, I just pick up a *jar of raspberry preserves, apricot jam, or lemon curd.* To make a sandwich, spread a little on the bottoms of two cookies. Then press the bottoms together into a sandwich. It's done!

I use a cream cheese frosting sometimes, flavored with some lemon zest, to stick two cookies together in a sandwich.

Crunchy peanut butter makes the perfect filling, too. ❞

PEPPERSASS COOKIES

Prep **30 MINUTES** *Bake* **10 MINUTES**

These are some of the most classic Christmas cookies of them all. Not surprisingly, they contain usually ground black pepper. Here's a brilliant new twist: use hot pepper sauce to flavor them up.

2¼	cups all-purpose flour
½	teaspoon baking soda
½	teaspoon salt
1	cup sugar plus additional for coating
⅔	cup butter or margarine, softened
1	large egg
2	teaspoons hot pepper sauce
1	teaspoon vanilla extract

LET'S BEGIN For the flour mixture, combine the first three ingredients in a medium bowl. Cream the sugar and butter in a large bowl with an electric mixer on medium speed until well blended. Add the egg, hot pepper sauce, vanilla, and flour mixture and beat until smooth.

CHILL IT Divide the dough in half and shape each piece into a log about 1½ inches in diameter. Wrap in plastic and refrigerate for at least 2 hours, or until firm.

SLICE & BAKE Preheat the oven to 350°F. Cut one log of dough into ¼-inch-thick slices. Dip each slice in sugar. Place 1 inch apart on ungreased cookie sheets. Bake for 10 to 12 minutes, until the cookies are golden around the edges. Transfer to wire racks to cool completely. Repeat with the remaining log.

Makes about 5 dozen cookies

Per cookie: 50 calories, 1g protein, 7g carbohydrates, 2g fat, 1g saturated fat, 9mg cholesterol, 54mg sodium

---

Time Savers

SPEEDING UP COOKIES

DOUBLE THE MIX

When measuring out the dry ingredients for your favorite cookies, make two batches. Bake up one and put the other batch in a resealable freezer bag. Store in a cabinet or other dry place. The next time you make cookies, you'll get in and out of the kitchen much faster.

NOT TOO COLD, PLEASE

Refrigerator cookie dough freezes well, up to three months. But when ready to bake, let it warm up about 15 minutes at room temperature. Saves baking time!

SPRAY IT!

Here's a tip to save you time when cutting slice 'n' bake cookie dough. Spray your knife with nonstick spray. Try it—slicing the cookie dough goes faster because the knife doesn't stick. The cookies will slice cleaner and bake up with smooth tops.

CRUMBS AWAY!

Place wire cooling rack on a clean cloth or piece of paper. Any crumbs from the cookies will fall on the cloth—not on the cabinet or floor. After cooling, just shake away the crumbs fast and save time cleaning.

LEMON CRISPS

Prep **1 HOUR + CHILLING**   *Bake* **8 MINUTES**

¾ cup unsalted butter, softened

1 cup sugar

1 large egg

1 tablespoon grated lemon zest

1½ cups all-purpose flour

Confectioners' sugar

It is easier to cut the dough log into thin slices when very cold. For the best results use a long, thin knife and cut straight down rather than saw back and forth.

LET'S BEGIN Cream the butter and sugar in a large bowl with an electric mixer on medium speed until light and fluffy. Add the egg and lemon zest and beat until well mixed. Reduce the speed to low and add the flour, beating until a soft dough forms.

CHILL IT Divide the dough in half. Shape each half into an 8-inch log (1½-inches in diameter) on a lightly floured surface. Wrap each log tightly in plastic. Refrigerate for 2 hours, or until firm.

SLICE & BAKE Preheat the oven to 350°F. Cut one log of dough into ⅛- to ¼-inch-thick slices. Place 1 inch apart on ungreased cookie sheets. Bake for 8 to 12 minutes, until the edges are very light brown. Let stand for 1 minute, then roll the cookies in confectioners' sugar while still warm. Transfer the cookies to wire racks to cool completely. Roll again in the sugar. Repeat with the remaining log.

Makes 6½ dozen cookies

Per cookie: 35 calories, 0g protein, 4g carbohydrates, 2g fat, 1g saturated fat, 8mg cholesterol, 1mg sodium

Sweetheart Kisses, page 131

Cookies on Holiday

What would holidays be without cookies? They seem to go together naturally. We've collected some of your favorites for our quick-cooking cookie baking: Mom's Butter Cookies, Linzer Heart Cookies, and Thumbprint Jewels. But that's just the start of our cookie surprises. We've transformed Easter eggs into cookies, flavored spritz cookies with browned butter, even made a Fourth-of-July pizza out of a giant cookie. Our recipes are high on flavor but low on work, for we've tucked in time-saving baking hints along the way. But the best part: You don't have to wait for a holiday to bake these. They're so buttery and delicious, they're good any time!

BE MY VALENTINE
Cut out the dough with a heart-shaped cutter. Sprinkle with red sugar and bake. Pipe red icing around the edge and a white heart in center.

LET IT SNOW, LET IT SNOW, LET IT SNOW
Cut out cookies with a snowflake cutter. Before baking, sprinkle with edible glitters in various colors or sanding sugar (look for them in gourmet cookware stores.)

IT'S BEGINNING TO LOOK A LOT LIKE CHRISTMAS
Cut out cookies with a tree-cutter. Bake, then paint with green icing. Sprinkle on edible glitter for garlands and tiny round candy for ornaments.

HOP ON DOWN!
Make giant Easter egg cookies. Cut out an oval piece of cardboard and use as a template for your cookies. Decorate some cookies with lilac, yellow, green, and pink icing in all of your favorite Easter egg patterns (for some ideas, see page 132).
Dip the others halfway in melted chocolate. Use glitter and colored sugars for decorations.

MOM'S BUTTER COOKIES

Prep **25 MINUTES + CHILLING**   *Bake* **8 MINUTES**

Butter cookies just don't get better than these. Lots of butter makes them very tender. Just be sure not to overmix the dough. Add a teaspoon of vanilla extract or a little lemon zest, if you like.

1	cup butter, softened
½	cup packed brown sugar
¼	cup granulated sugar
2	cups all-purpose flour

LET'S BEGIN Combine the butter, brown sugar, and granulated sugar in a large bowl. Beat with an electric mixer on medium speed until light and fluffy. Reduce the speed to low and blend in the flour until well blended.

CHILL IT Divide the dough in half. Wrap each half in plastic and flatten into a disk. Refrigerate for at least 1 hour, or until firm, but not hard.

ROLL & BAKE Preheat the oven to 350°F. Roll out one piece of the dough on a lightly floured surface to a ⅛-inch thickness (keeping remaining dough refrigerated). Cut out cookies with 3-inch cutters. Place 1 inch apart on ungreased cookie sheets. Repeat with the remaining dough. Bake for 8 to 10 minutes, until the edges are very light brown. Transfer to wire racks to cool completely.

Makes 4 dozen cookies
Per cookie: 65 calories, 1g protein, 7g carbohydrates, 4g fat, 3g saturated fat, 10mg cholesterol, 42mg sodium

SuperQuick

CAROLING COOKIES

Prep **20 MINUTES**   *Bake* **10 MINUTES**

2½   cups all-purpose flour

1   teaspoon baking soda

1   teaspoon cream of tartar

1   package (10 ounces)
      white chips

⅔   cup butter or margarine,
      softened

⅔   cup sugar

2   large eggs

1   teaspoon vanilla extract

1   package (10 ounces)
      holiday candy bits

It's beginning to look like Christmas—and music is in the air. Greet the carolers with these festive cookies, decorated with the colors of the season. Make a double batch, as they freeze swell.

LET'S BEGIN Preheat the oven to 325°F. Combine the flour, baking soda, and cream of tartar in a bowl. Melt 1 cup of the white chips.

MIX IT IN Cream the butter, sugar, eggs, and vanilla in a large bowl with an electric mixer on medium speed until light and fluffy. Beat in the melted chips. Stir in the remaining chips and the candy bits.

DROP & BAKE Drop rounded teaspoonfuls of the dough 2 inches apart on ungreased cookie sheets. Bake for 10 to 12 minutes, until very light brown. Transfer to racks to cool.

Makes 4 dozen cookies

Per cookie: 120 calories, 1g protein, 16g carbohydrates, 6g fat, 4g saturated fat, 17mg cholesterol, 69mg sodium

RUSSIAN TEA CAKES

Prep **45 MINUTES**   *Bake* **18 MINUTES**

1	**cup butter, softened**
¼	**cup granulated sugar**
1	**teaspoon vanilla extract**
2	**cups all-purpose flour**
2	**cups finely chopped pecans or walnuts**

Confectioners' sugar

These little round cookies look just like mini-snowballs.

LET'S BEGIN Preheat the oven to 325°F. Cream butter, granulated sugar, and vanilla in a large bowl on medium speed of an electric mixer until light. Reduce speed to low and blend in the flour. Stir in the nuts. Roll into 1-inch balls.

DROP & BAKE Place cookies 1 inch apart on ungreased cookie sheets. Bake for 18 to 25 minutes, until very light brown. Cool for 5 minutes. Roll in confectioners' sugar while warm. Transfer to wire racks. Roll cookies again when cool.

Makes 3 dozen cookies

Per cookie: 130 calories, 1g protein, 11g carbohydrates, 10g fat, 4g saturated fat, 15mg cholesterol, 50mg sodium

MOONBEAM COOKIES

Prep **30 MINUTES**   *Bake* **9 MINUTES**   *Microwave* **2 MINUTES**

1	**package (18 ounces) refrigerated sugar cookies**
1	**cup coconut**
½	**cup lemon curd**
2	**ounces vanilla-flavored candy coating or ⅓ cup white vanilla chips**

These cookies taste so terrific that no one will ever guess they're made with only four ingredients and very little effort.

LET'S BEGIN Preheat oven to 350°F. Break up the cookie dough in a large bowl and stir in the coconut. Shape into 1-inch balls and place 2 inches apart on ungreased cookie sheets. Use your thumb or the handle of a wooden spoon to make an indentation in the center of each cookie. Fill each with about ½ teaspoon of the lemon curd.

INTO THE OVEN Bake cookies for 10 to 13 minutes, or just until edges are light golden brown.Cool on a wire rack for 5 minutes. Microwave candy coating in a small microwavable bowl on Medium for 2 minutes. Stir. Drizzle over cookies.

Makes 3 dozen cookies

Per cookie: 89 calories, 1g protein, 11g carbohydrates, 5g fat, 2g saturated fat, 4mg cholesterol, 75mg sodium

BROWNED-BUTTER SPRITZ

Prep **45** MINUTES   *Chill* **45** MINUTES   *Bake* **8** MINUTES

2¼   cups all-purpose flour

½   teaspoon baking powder

¼   teaspoon salt

1   cup butter

¾   cup granulated sugar

1   large egg

1   teaspoon vanilla extract

1   to 2 tablespoons milk

Decorator sugars (optional)

Who doesn't love buttery spritz cookies? These are the best ever as they are made with nutty-tasting brown butter. Bake up a batch and get ready to trim the tree.

LET'S BEGIN Combine the flour, baking powder, and salt in a medium bowl. Melt the butter in a small heavy saucepan over medium heat, then continue cooking, stirring constantly, until the butter turns a deep rich brown. Immediately pour the butter into a medium metal bowl. Cover and refrigerate for 45 minutes, or until the butter is cool to the touch and slightly solid.

MIX IT IN Preheat the oven to 375°F. Spoon the butter into a large bowl and add the sugar. Beat with an electric mixer on medium speed until light and fluffy. Add the egg and vanilla and beat until well mixed. Reduce the speed to low and beat in the flour mixture and 1 tablespoon of the milk until well blended. (If the dough seems dry, add the remaining 1 tablespoon milk.)

INTO THE OVEN Fit a cookie press with the desired template and fill with the cookie dough. Press cookies about 2 inches apart onto ungreased cookie sheets. Sprinkle with decorator sugars, if you like. Bake for 8 to 10 minutes, until the edges are light brown. Transfer the cookies to wire racks to cool completely.

Makes 6 dozen cookies

Per cookie: 48 calories, 1g protein, 5g carbohydrates, 3g fat, 2g saturated fat, 10mg cholesterol, 40mg sodium

CANDY CANE COOKIES

Prep **40 MINUTES**   *Bake* **9 MINUTES**

1   cup unsalted butter, softened

1   cup confectioners' sugar

1   large egg yolk

1½   teaspoons vanilla extract

2½   cups all-purpose flour

1   teaspoon salt

½   teaspoon red food coloring

½   cup peppermint candy, crushed

¼   cup blanched almonds (whole, sliced, or slivered), ground

¼   cup granulated sugar

These look like candy canes but taste like buttery cookies. The secret to getting the stripes just right is to twist the white and red pieces of dough tightly—like a rope.

LET'S BEGIN Preheat the oven to 375°F. Cream the butter, confectioners' sugar, egg yolk, and vanilla in a large bowl with an electric mixer on medium speed until light. Reduce the speed to low and beat in the flour and salt until blended. Divide the dough in half. Mix the red food coloring and ¼ cup of the crushed peppermint candy into one half, then mix the ground almonds into the other half.

ROLL & SHAPE Break off 1 heaping teaspoonful each of red dough and white dough. Roll each piece into a 4-inch-long rope. Place them side by side, pinch the ends together, and twist them to form a rope. Place on ungreased cookie sheets and curve the top ends to form candy canes. Repeat with the remaining dough.

BAKE & SPRINKLE Bake for 9 minutes, or until the cookies just begin to brown. Toss the remaining ¼ cup peppermint candy and the granulated sugar in a small bowl. Sprinkle the warm cookies with peppermint-sugar mixture, then transfer to wire racks to cool completely.

Makes 4 dozen cookies
Per cookie: 157 calories, 2g protein, 18g carbohydrates, 7g fat, 5g saturated fat, 29mg cholesterol, 157mg sodium

Fun Gingerbread Cutouts

Prep **45 MINUTES**   *Chill* **2 HOURS**   *Bake* **7 MINUTES**

COOKIES

1	package (18¼ ounces) spice cake mix
¾	cup butter, softened
1	large egg
2	tablespoons orange juice or milk
1	teaspoon ground cinnamon
1	teaspoon vanilla extract
½	teaspoon ground ginger

FROSTING

4½	cups confectioners' sugar
⅓	cup butter, softened
2	tablespoons orange juice or milk
2	to 3 tablespoons milk

Assorted food colors, if you wish

Color these cutouts any season you wish—pastels for spring birthdays; red, green, and white for Christmas.

LET'S BEGIN Beat half of the cake mix and all remaining cookie ingredients in a large bowl with an electric mixer on low speed for 2 to 3 minutes, scraping often. Beat in remaining cake mix for 1 to 2 minutes more or until well mixed. Wrap in plastic food wrap and refrigerate until firm, at least 2 hours.

ROLL & CUT Preheat oven to 375° F. Roll out dough, half at a time, on a lightly floured surface to ⅛-inch thickness. Cut out cookies with 3- to 4-inch cutters. Place on ungreased cookie sheets 2 inches apart and bake for 7 to 9 minutes or until set. Let stand 1 minute, and cool completely on wire racks.

DECORATE Beat all of the frosting ingredients except milk and food colors on low speed, adding enough milk for spreading consistency. Spread on cookies and decorate as you wish.

Makes 2 dozen cookies
Per cookie: 240 calories, 2g protein, 35g carbohydrates, 11g fat, 6g saturated fat, 35mg cholesterol, 230mg sodium

THUMBPRINT JEWELS

Prep **25 MINUTES + CHILLING**   *Bake* **16 MINUTES**

1   cup unsalted butter,
      softened

½   cup granulated sugar

¼   teaspoon salt

2   large egg yolks

1   teaspoon vanilla extract

3   cups all-purpose flour

Superfine sugar for rolling
(optional)

Assorted jams and jellies,
such as strawberry and
raspberry

Calling all thumbs! Half the fun of these classic buttery cookies is making an indentation in each one. For a colorful assortment, use raspberry, blueberry, and orange preserves.

LET'S BEGIN Cream the butter, sugar, and salt in a large bowl with an electric mixer on medium-high speed until light and fluffy Add the egg yolks and vanilla and beat until the mixture is very light. Reduce the speed to low and add the flour in three additions, beating just until the flour is no longer visible. (Do not overbeat or the cookies will be tough.) Cover the bowl and refrigerate for 1 to 2 hours, until firm.

EASY ROLL Preheat the oven to 375°F. Grease two cookie sheets. Roll the dough into ¾-inch balls. Roll each ball in superfine sugar until coated, if you like. Place the balls about 1 inch apart on cookie sheets. Make an indentation in each ball with your thumb.

INTO THE OVEN Bake the cookies for 16 to 18 minutes, just until light brown (do not overbake). Transfer the cookies to wire racks to cool completely. Store in an airtight container. Before serving, fill the centers of the cookies with a spoonful of jam or jelly.

Makes about 6 dozen cookies
Per cookie: 48 calories, 1g protein, 5g carbohydrates, 3g fat, 2g saturated fat, 13mg cholesterol, 33mg sodium

FROSTED PEPPARKAKOR

Prep **1 HOUR**   *Chill* **1 HOUR**   *Bake* **5 MINUTES**

2   cups all-purpose flour

½   teaspoon salt

½   teaspoon baking soda

½   teaspoon ground cinnamon

½   teaspoon ground ginger

½   teaspoon ground nutmeg

½   cup butter, softened

½   cup firmly packed brown sugar

½   cup light molasses

Royal Icing (see page 133, optional)

These traditional molasses spiced cookies are from Sweden are usually made in fancy heart shapes. Try the same dough for cutting out gingerbread people too, rolling the dough ⅛-inch thick.

LET'S BEGIN Preheat oven to 375°F. Mix the first 6 ingredients in a medium bowl and set aside.

MIX IT UP Cream the butter, brown sugar, and molasses with an electric mixer on medium speed until light. Reduce speed to low an blend in the flour. Form into two 5-inch disks, wrap, and chill for at least 1 hour, or until firm.

ROLL & BAKE Preheat oven to 375°F. Roll out the dough on a lightly floured surface, to 1/16 thick, (keep remaining dough refrigerated). Cut with 2- to 2½-inch heart-shaped cutters. Place 1 inch apart onto ungreased cookie sheets. Bake for 5 to 7 minutes, or just until set. Transfer to wire racks to cool. Decorate with Royal Icing, if you wish.

Makes 6 dozen cookies
Per cookie: 35 calories, 1g protein, 8g carbohydrates, 1.5g fat, 1g saturated fat, 4mg cholesterol, 40mg sodium

LINZER HEART COOKIES

Prep **40 MINUTES + CHILLING**   *Bake* **12 MINUTES**

2⅓   cups all-purpose flour

½   cup ground almonds

1   tablespoon pumpkin pie spice

1   teaspoon baking powder

½   teaspoon salt

1   cup unsalted butter or margarine, softened

¾   cup granulated sugar

2   large eggs

1   teaspoon vanilla extract

Confectioners' sugar for dusting

⅔   cup raspberry preserves

Nothing says "I love you" more than these delectable raspberry-filled heart-shaped sandwich cookies. Pumpkin pie spice is an aromatic mix of all the spices needed.

LET'S BEGIN For flour mixture, stir the first five ingredients together in a medium bowl. Cream the butter and granulated sugar in a large bowl with an electric mixer on medium speed until light and fluffy. Beat in the eggs, one at a time, then the vanilla. Reduce the speed to low and blend in the flour mixture. Divide the dough in half, pat each piece into a disk, and wrap in plastic. Refrigerate for 3 to 4 hours, or until firm.

ROLL & BAKE Preheat the oven to 375°F. Grease two cookie sheets or line with parchment paper. Roll one piece of dough out on a lightly floured surface to a ⅛-inch thickness. Cut into hearts using a 2½-inch cutter. Using a 1-inch heart-shaped cutter, cut out the centers of half of the hearts. Repeat with the second piece of dough, rerolling the cut-out centers and scraps of dough. Place hearts on the cookie sheets about 1 inch apart, putting all of the solid hearts on one sheet and hearts without centers on another sheet. Bake until light golden brown, about 9 minutes for the hearts without centers and about 12 minutes for the solid hearts. Transfer to wire racks to cool completely.

DECORATE Using a small strainer, sift confectioners' sugar over the hearts without centers. Spread the tops of the solid hearts with raspberry preserves, leaving a ¼-inch border all around. Top each with a cut-out "sugared" heart.

Makes about 3 dozen cookies
Per cookie: 127 calories, 2g protein, 15g carbohydrates, 7g fat, 4g saturated fat, 26mg cholesterol, 49mg sodium

SWEETHEART KISSES

Prep **25 MINUTES**   *Bake* **ABOUT 15 MINUTES**   *Microwave* **2 MINUTES**

**Sugar-cookie dough
(purchased or made from
your favorite recipe)**

**Unsweetened cocoa
for dusting**

**48   milk chocolate kisses,
unwrapped**

**1   teaspoon vegetable
shortening (not butter,
margarine spread, or oil)**

*Be sure to have extra chocolate kisses on hand because some will
surely be snatched for snacking. Won't you be my valentine?*

LET'S BEGIN Preheat the oven as directed on package or
in recipe. Divide the dough in half. Roll out one half at a time
to a ¼-inch thickness.

INTO THE OVEN Cut out cookies with 2-inch heart-
shaped cutters and place on ungreased cookie sheets. Bake
according to package or recipe directions. Transfer to wire
racks to cool completely. Put some cocoa into a small strainer
and dust the cookies.

DECORATE Place 12 chocolate kisses and the shortening
in a small microwavable bowl. Microwave on High for
1 minute, then microwave on High for 15-second intervals,
stirring until melted and smooth. Drizzle over the cookies.
Before the chocolate sets, place a chocolate kiss in the center
of each heart.

Makes about 3 dozen cookies

*Per cookie: 102 calories, 1g protein, 12g carbohydrates,
5g fat, 2g saturated fat, 6mg cholesterol, 66mg sodium*

Time Savers

CUT OUT CUTTING TIME

Here's a way to save valuable
minutes when making the
Linzer Heart Cookies. Cut out
an equal number of hearts in
two different sizes: 2½ and
1 inch. (Save time by not cutting out the centers from the
larger hearts.) Bake as directed.

After baking and cooling the
hearts, sprinkle the small hearts
with confectioners' sugar. To
"fill," spread the tops of the
larger hearts with the raspberry
preserves. Top each large heart
with a small heart in the center.
Give to your sweetheart!

EASTER EGG COOKIES

Prep **30 MINUTES + CHILLING**   *Bake* **10 MINUTES**

½   cup butter, softened

⅓   cup granulated sugar

2   teaspoons milk

1   cup all-purpose flour

½   cup sweetened flaked coconut

Edible glitter and decorator sugars (optional)

Get out your favorite Easter basket and fill it with these luscious morsels. Edible glitter is available in a multitude of colors in cake-decorating stores.

LET'S BEGIN Cream the butter and sugar in a large bowl with an electric mixer on medium speed until light and fluffy. Beat in the milk until well mixed. Reduce the speed to low and add the flour, beating until well blended. Stir in the coconut with a wooden spoon.

CHILL IT Wrap the dough in plastic and refrigerate for 1 to 2 hours, until firm.

DROP & BAKE Preheat the oven to 325°F. Shape rounded teaspoonfuls of the dough into 1 × ¾-inch egg shapes. Roll each cookie in edible glitter and decorator sugar, if you like. Place about 1 inch apart on ungreased cookie sheets. Bake for 10 to 12 minutes, until the bottoms are light brown. Transfer the cookies to wire racks to cool completely.

Makes 4 dozen cookies

Per cookie: 38 calories, 0g protein, 4g carbohydrates, 2g fat, 2g saturated fat, 6mg cholesterol, 25mg sodium

---

Cook to Cook

HOW DO I GET MY COOKIE ICING TO LOOK SMOOTH?

"I use *Royal Icing, also called Decorator's Icing.* It's perfect for decorating cookies, even cakes. It's simple to make. *The traditional recipe* calls for beating an egg white until stiff and then adding 1¼ cups sifted confectioners' sugar, ¼ teaspoon cream of tartar, and 2 tablespoons water in a bowl. Because I prefer not to use raw egg whites, *I replace the egg with 1 tablespoon meringue powder.*

Then, I beat all the ingredients on low speed with an electric mixer, until combined, then on high speed until stiff and glossy. Don't be shy about adding in a bit more water, if you need it. I then tint it with food colors and spoon it into a pastry bag fitted with a tiny tip. Then just pipe away! Or, if you wish, add a few more drops of water and paint it on the cookies with a small brush."

FOURTH OF JULY COOKIE PIZZA

Prep **25 MINUTES + COOLING**   *Bake* **14 MINUTES**

1   package (18 ounces) refrigerated sugar-cookie dough

½   cup heavy cream

1   container (8 ounces) low-fat vanilla yogurt

1   pint California strawberries, stemmed and halved

1   cup fresh blueberries

Time to celebrate! Here's a great idea. Make individual pizzas (on small pizza pans or in disposable pie or tart tins) and let guests decorate their own as creatively as they like.

LET'S BEGIN Preheat the oven to 350°F. Butter and flour the bottom and side of a 14-inch pizza pan. With floured hands, press the cookie dough evenly onto the bottom of the pan.

INTO THE OVEN Bake in the center of the oven for 14 to 16 minutes, until golden brown. Run a narrow metal spatula or thin knife along the edge of crust to loosen it from the pan. Place the crust in the pan on a wire rack to cool completely.

DECORATE Beat the cream in a medium bowl until soft peaks form. Fold the yogurt into the cream. Cover and refrigerate up to several hours, if desired. Just before serving, spread the cream mixture evenly over the crust. Decorate with the strawberries and blueberries. Cut into wedges and serve.

Makes 12 wedges

Per wedge: 250 calories, 3g protein, 32g carbohydrates, 13g fat, 5g saturated fat, 25 mg cholesterol, 200mg sodium

---

Cook to Cook

WHAT'S ANOTHER WAY TO DECORATE A COOKIE PIZZA?

"I like to top my pizza with an American Flag for the Fourth. Here's how. *Frost the pizza* with about three-fourths of the yogurt-cream mixture as directed above. *Outline a flag shape* with a wooden pick. Fill the upper left-hand corner with blueberries. Arrange two rows of thickly sliced strawberries across the top of the flag (making a red stripe). Leave an equal-size space of white under the red stripe (making a white stripe). Continue alternating red and white stripes. *To create stars,* put the remaining cream mixture into a pastry bag fitted with a star tip and pipe stars on top of the blueberries."

HALLOWEEN COOKIES ON A STICK

Prep **25** MINUTES   *Bake* **10** MINUTES

2½   **cups all-purpose flour**

⅓   **cup cocoa**

1   **teaspoon baking soda**

½   **teaspoon salt**

1   **cup butter or margarine, softened**

¾   **cup granulated sugar**

¾   **cup packed light brown sugar**

1   **teaspoons vanilla extract**

2   **large eggs**

18   **wooden ice cream sticks**

Royal Icing (see page 133, optional)

Spooks and goblins that are great to eat—and perfect for your next Halloween party. Let the kids decorate their own.

LET'S BEGIN Preheat the oven to 350°F. For the flour mixture, combine the flour, cocoa, baking soda, and salt in a large bowl. Set aside.

MIX IT UP Beat the butter, granulated sugar, brown sugar, and vanilla in a large bowl with an electric mixer on medium speed until light. Beat in the eggs. Reduce the speed to low and gradually add the flour mixture until well blended.

DROP & BAKE Drop scant ¼ cupfuls of the dough about 3 inches apart on an ungreased cookie sheet. Shape into balls, insert a wooden stick about halfway into the center of each, and flatten slightly. Bake for 10 to 12 minutes, until set. Cool for 3 minutes, then carefully transfer the cookies to a wire rack to cool completely. Decorate as desired with decorating icing.

Makes 18 cookies

Per cookie: 53 calories, 3g protein, 31g carbohydrates, 12g fat, 7g saturated fat, 53mg cholesterol, 256mg sodium

JACK-'O-LANTERN BARS

Prep **15 MINUTES + COOLING**   *Bake* **25 MINUTES**

BARS

2	cups all-purpose flour
2	cups granulated sugar
2	teaspoons pumpkin pie spice
2	teaspoons baking powder
1	teaspoon baking soda
½	teaspoon salt
4	large eggs, lightly beaten
1	can (15 ounces) solid-pack pumpkin
1	cup vegetable oil

FROSTING

2	cups confectioners' sugar
1	package (3 ounces) cream cheese, softened
⅓	cup butter or margarine, softened
1	tablespoon milk
1	teaspoon vanilla extract
3	drops yellow food color
2	drops red food color

DECORATIONS

Candy corn (optional)

If you don't have pumpkin pie spice blend on hand for these bars, mix 1 teaspoon ground cinnamon, ½ teaspoon ground nutmeg, and ¼ teaspoon each of ground ginger and cloves.

LET'S BEGIN Preheat the oven to 350°F. Butter and flour a 15 × 10-inch jelly-roll pan. To make the bars, combine the first six ingredients in a medium bowl.

MIX IT UP Add the eggs, pumpkin, and oil, stirring until well blended. Pour into the pan and spread evenly. Bake for 25 to 30 minutes, until a wooden pick inserted in the center comes out clean. Transfer the bars in the pan to a wire rack to cool completely.

DECORATE Mix the frosting ingredients in a small bowl until smooth. Spread over the cooled bars with a narrow metal spatula. Cut into squares and decorate as desired.

Makes 2 dozen bars

Per cookie: 275 calories, 3g protein, 36g carbohydrates, 14g fat, 4g saturated fat, 46mg cholesterol, 184mg sodium

SPICED SUGAR COOKIES

Prep **30 MINUTES + CHILLING**   *Bake* **10 MINUTES**

3½   cups all-purpose flour

2   teaspoons ground ginger

2   teaspoons ground cinnamon

1   teaspoon ground black pepper

½   teaspoon baking powder

½   teaspoon salt

¾   cup unsalted butter, softened

⅔   cup vegetable shortening

¾   cup granulated sugar

1   large egg

¼   teaspoon vanilla extract

½   cup milk chocolate–hazelnut spread

2½   tablespoons milk

2   tablespoons confectioners' sugar, sifted

Candy decorations, jimmies, sprinkles, mini chips, and assorted Halloween candy (optional)

It'll be hard not to dip a finger into the milk chocolate–hazelnut spread for a taste or two. It makes a quick and fabulous frosting. Great for frosting cupcakes, too.

LET'S BEGIN For the flour mixture, combine the first six ingredients in a medium bowl. Cream the butter, shortening, and sugar in a large bowl with an electric mixer on medium-high speed until light and fluffy. Beat in the egg and vanilla. Reduce the speed to low and gradually blend in the flour mixture just until combined. Divide the dough in half, and flatten each piece into a disk. Wrap in plastic and refrigerate for 1 hour, or until firm.

ROLL & BAKE Preheat the oven to 375°F. Grease two cookie sheets. Roll one piece of dough out on a lightly floured surface or on waxed paper to a ⅛-inch thickness. Cut out desired cookies with bats, pumpkin, or headstone cutters and place on a cookie sheet. Repeat with the remaining dough. Bake for 10 minutes. Transfer to a wire rack to cool completely.

DECORATE Combine the hazelnut spread, milk, and confectioners' sugar in a small saucepan and cook, stirring, over low heat until slightly warm. Spread over the top of each cookie and decorate as desired.

Makes 2 dozen cookies
Per cookie: 233 calories, 2g protein, 25g carbohydrates, 14g fat, 6g saturated fat, 26mg cholesterol, 64mg sodium

CREDITS

PAGE 2 Duncan Hines: Photo for Peanut Butter Knockouts courtesy of Duncan Hines. Used with permission.

PAGE 8 Land O'Lakes: Photo for Pistachio-White Chocolate Chip Cookies courtesy of Land O'Lakes, Inc. Used with permission.

PAGE 13 Ocean Spray Cranberries: Photo for Chocolate-dipped Cranberry Cookies courtesy of Ocean Spray Cranberries, Inc. Used with permission.

PAGE 16 Kraft Foods: Photo for Fruit & Nut Cookies courtesy of Kraft Kitchens. Used with permission.

PAGE 18/19 Swans Down: Recipe and photo for Ultimate Chocolate Chip Oatmeal Cookies courtesy of Swans Down Cake Flour. Used with permission.

PAGE 20/21 Kraft Foods: Recipe and photo for Sour Cream Chocolate Chip Cookies courtesy of Kraft Kitchens. Used with permission.

PAGE 22 Nutella: Recipe for Stix 'n' Stones courtesy of Ferrero USA, manufacturer of Nutella hazelnut spread. Used with permission.

PAGE 23 Domino: Recipe for Thimble Cookies courtesy of Domino Sugar. Used with permission.

PAGE 24 Cherry Marketing Institute: Recipe for Sweetie Pies courtesy of The Cherry Marketing Institute. Used with permission.

PAGE 25 Hershey Foods: Recipe for Lemon Butter Pecan Cookies courtesy of Hershey Kitchens, Hershey Foods Corporation, Hershey, PA. Used with permission.

PAGE 26 Ocean Spray Cranberries: Recipe and photo for Black Forest Cookies courtesy of Ocean Spray Cranberries, Inc. Used with permission.

PAGE 27 Sun-Maid: Recipe for Classic Oatmeal-Raisin Cookies courtesy of Sun-Maid Growers of California. Used with permission.

PAGE 28/29 Dole: Recipe and photo for Pineapple-Oatmeal "Scotchies" courtesy of Dole Food Company. Used with permission.

PAGE 30 Sunkist: Recipe for B-I-G Fruit & Oatmeal Cookies courtesy of Sunkist Growers, Inc. Used with permission.

PAGE 31 Wisconsin Milk Marketing Board: Recipe and photo for Cheddar-Apple Kickoff Cookies courtesy of the Wisconsin Milk Marketing Board, Inc. Used with permission.

PAGE 32 Kraft Foods: Recipe and photo for Fruit & Nut Cookies courtesy of Kraft Kitchens. Used with permission.

PAGE 33 Swans Down: Recipe for Drop Sugar Cookies courtesy of Swans Down Cake Flour. Used with permission.

PAGE 34 Land O'Lakes: Recipe and photo for Snickerdoodles courtesy of Land O'Lakes, Inc. Used with permission.

PAGE 35 Domino: Recipe for Ginger Melts courtesy of Domino Sugar. Used with permission.

PAGE 36/37 Duncan Hines: Recipe and photo for Peanut Butter Knockouts courtesy of Duncan Hines. Used with permission.

PAGE 38 Land O'Lakes: Recipe for Okeechobee Bobbers courtesy of Land O'Lakes, Inc. Used with permission.

PAGE 39 Land O'Lakes: Recipe for Chinese Almond Cookies courtesy of Land O'Lakes, Inc. Used with permission.

PAGE 40/42 Kraft Foods: Recipe and photo for Banana Snack Bars courtesy of Kraft Kitchens. Used with permission.

PAGE 42/43 Kraft Foods: Recipe and photo for Fruity Carb Bars courtesy of Kraft Kitchens. Used with permission.

PAGE 44 National Sunflower Association: Recipe and photo for Sunflower & Cranberry Granola Bars courtesy of the National Sunflower Association. Used with permission.

PAGE 45 Cherry Marketing Institute: Recipe and photo for Wholesome Granola Bars courtesy of The Cherry Marketing Institute. Used with permission.

PAGE 46 Land O'Lakes: Recipe for Maple-Butter Pecan Shortbread courtesy of Land O'Lakes, Inc. Used with permission.

PAGE 47 Birds Eye: Recipe for Raspberry Shortbread Bars courtesy of Birds Eye Foods. Used with permission.

PAGE 48 Domino: Recipe and photo for Raspberry & Cream Cheese Bars courtesy of Domino Sugar. Used with permission.

PAGE 49 Land O'Lakes: Recipe for Rocky Road Brownies courtesy of Land O'Lakes, Inc. Used with permission.

PAGE 50/51 Duncan Hines: Recipe and photo for Yummy Peanut Butter Bars courtesy of Duncan Hines. Used with permission.

PAGE 51 Kraft Foods: Recipe for Zap-It Bars courtesy of Kraft Kitchens. Used with permission.

PAGE 52 Quaker: Recipe and photo for Blueberry Streusel Squares courtesy of The Quaker Oats Company. Used with permission.

PAGE 53 Quaker: Recipe for Chunky Chocolate Blonde Brownies courtesy of The Quaker Oats Company. Used with permission.

PAGE 54/55 Duncan Hines: Recipe and photo for Chocolate Chip Caramel Bars courtesy of Duncan Hines. Used with permission.

PAGE 56 Domino: Recipe for Brown Sugar & Apple Bars courtesy of Domino Sugar. Used with permission.

PAGE 57 Dole: Recipe for Caramel Pineapple Bar Cookies courtesy of Dole Food Company. Used with permission.

PAGE 58/59 Land O'Lakes: Recipe and photo for Double-Lemon Bars courtesy of Land O'Lakes, Inc. Used with permission.

PAGE 60 Hershey Foods: Recipe and photo for Our Very Best Brownies courtesy of Hershey Kitchens, Hershey Foods Corporation, Hershey, PA. Used with permission.

PAGE 61 Domino: Recipe for Caramel-Pecan Brownies courtesy of Domino Sugar. Used with permission.

PAGE 62 Kraft Foods: Photo for Little Ladies courtesy of Kraft Kitchens. Used with permission.

PAGE 64 Land O'Lakes: Recipe and photo for Gum Drop Cookies courtesy of Land O'Lakes, Inc. Used with permission.

PAGE 65 Birds Eye: Recipe for Ruby Cowboy Cookies courtesy of Birds Eye Foods. Used with permission.

PAGE 66/67 Dole: Recipe and photo for Lollipop Cookies courtesy of Dole Food Company. Used with permission.

PAGE 68 Skippy: Recipe for Peanut Gobblers courtesy of Unilever Best Foods. Used with permission. © 2004 Unilever Bestfoods.

PAGE 69 Cherry Marketing Institute: Recipe and photo for Cherry Chews courtesy of The Cherry Marketing Institute. Used with permission.

PAGE 70 Kraft Foods: Recipe and photo for Little Ladies courtesy of Kraft Kitchens. Used with permission.

PAGE 71 Domino: Recipe for Apple-K-Dabbers courtesy of Domino Sugar. Used with permission.

PAGE 72 Land O'Lakes: Recipe for MMM-Good Cookies courtesy of Land O'Lakes, Inc. Used with permission.

PAGE 72/73 Hershey Foods: Recipe for Ooodle-Kadoodles courtesy of Hershey Kitchens, Hershey Foods Corporation, Hershey, PA. Used with permission.

PAGE 74 Hershey Foods: Recipe and photo for S'mores courtesy of Hershey Kitchens, Hershey Foods Corporation, Hershey, PA. Used with permission.

PAGE 75 Hershey Foods: Recipe and photo for Chocolate Teddy Bears courtesy of Hershey Kitchens, Hershey Foods Corporation, Hershey, PA. Used with permission.

PAGE 76 Hershey Foods: Recipe and photo for Peanut Blossoms courtesy of Hershey Kitchens, Hershey Foods Corporation, Hershey, PA. Used with permission.

PAGE 77 Hershey Foods: Recipe and photo for Chocolate X's & O's courtesy of Hershey Kitchens, Hershey Foods Corporation, Hershey, PA. Used with permission.

PAGE 78/79 Kraft Foods: Recipe and photo for Nutty Mallow Grahamwiches courtesy of Kraft Kitchens. Used with permission.

PAGE 79 National Association of Margarine Manufacturers: Recipe for S'more Bars courtesy of the National Association of Margarine Manufacturers. Used with permission.

PAGE 80 Land O'Lakes: Recipe and photo for Chocolate Caramel & Nut Treats courtesy of Land O'Lakes, Inc. Used with permission.

PAGE 81 Land O'Lakes: Recipe and photo for Jimmy Jumbles courtesy of Land O'Lakes, Inc. Used with permission.

PAGE 82 Hershey Foods: Recipe and photo for Classic Chocolate Chips courtesy of Hershey Kitchens, Hershey Foods Corporation, Hershey, PA. Used with permission.

PAGE 83 Quaker: Recipe and photo for Peanut Marbles courtesy of The Quaker Oats Company. Used with permission.

PAGE 84 Duncan Hines: Photo for Chocolate Macadamia Cookies courtesy of Duncan Hines. Used with permission.

PAGE 86 Kraft Foods: Recipe for Divine Truffle Brownies courtesy of Kraft Kitchens. Used with permission.

PAGE 87 Hershey Foods: Recipe and photo for White Chip Brownies courtesy of Hershey Kitchens, Hershey Foods Corporation, Hershey, PA. Used with permission.

PAGE 88/89 Kraft Foods: Recipe and photo for Chocolate Toffee Bars courtesy of Kraft Kitchens. Used with permission.

PAGE 90 Kraft Foods: Recipe for Chocolate-Coconut Pecan Squares courtesy of Kraft Foods. Used with permission.

PAGE 91 Kraft Foods: Recipe for Layered Chocolate-Peanut Butter Bars courtesy of Kraft Foods. Used with permission.

PAGE 92/93 Quaker: Recipe and photo for Chocolate-Raspberry Squares courtesy of The Quaker Oats Company. Used with permission.

PAGE 94 Hershey Foods: Recipe for Doubly Chocolate Cookies courtesy of Hershey Kitchens, Hershey Foods Corporation, Hershey, PA. Used with permission.

PAGE 95 Duncan Hines: Recipe for Chocolate Macadamia Cookies courtesy of Duncan Hines. Used with permission.

PAGE 95 Quaker: Recipe for No-Bake Chocolate Cookies courtesy of The Quaker Oats Company. Used with permission.

PAGE 96/97 Sugar in the Raw: Recipe and photo for Chocolate Brownie Cookies courtesy of Sugar In The Raw(r), a registered trademark of Cumberland Packing Corporation. Used with permission.

PAGE 98/99 Ocean Spray Cranberries: Recipe and photo for Chocolate-dipped Cranberry Cookies courtesy of Ocean Spray Cranberries, Inc. Used with permission.

PAGE 100/101 Land O'Lakes: Recipe and photo for Pistachio White Chocolate Chip Cookies courtesy of Land O'Lakes, Inc. Used with permission.

PAGE 102 Kraft Foods: Recipe for Apricot & Cranberry White Chocolate Chunks courtesy of Kraft Kitchens. Used with permission.

PAGE 103 Land O'Lakes: Recipe for Chocolate-dipped Hearts courtesy of Land O'Lakes, Inc. Used with permission.

PAGE 104/105 Land O'Lakes: Recipe and photo for Mexican Chocolate Wedding Cakes courtesy of Land O'Lakes, Inc. Used with permission.

PAGE 105 Domino: Recipe for Chocolate Truffle Snowballs courtesy of Domino Sugar. Used with permission.

PAGE 106/107 Kraft Foods: Recipe and photo for Chocolate Pudding Cookies courtesy of Kraft Kitchens. Used with permission.

WEBSITES

PAGE 108 Land O'Lakes: Photo for Chocolate Pinwheels courtesy of Land O'Lakes, Inc. Used with permission.

PAGE 110 Land O'Lakes: Recipe for Browned-Butter Cream Sandwich Cookies courtesy of Land O'Lakes, Inc. Used with permission.

PAGE 111 Land O'Lakes: Recipe for Chocolate Pinwheels courtesy of Land O'Lakes, Inc. Used with permission.

PAGE 112/113 Land O'Lakes: Recipe and photo for Melt-in-Your-Mouth Shortbread courtesy of Land O'Lakes, Inc. Used with permission.

PAGE 114 Domino: Recipe for Chocolate-dipped Refrigerator Cookies courtesy of Domino Sugar. Used with permission.

PAGE 115 McCormick: Recipe for Spiced Icebox Cookies courtesy of McCormick. Used with permission.

PAGE 116 McIlhenny Company: Recipe for Peppersass Cookies courtesy of McIlhenny Company. Used with permission.

PAGE 117 Land O'Lakes: Recipe for Lemon Crisps courtesy of Land O'Lakes, Inc. Used with permission.

PAGE 118 Hershey Foods: Photo for Sweetheart Kisses courtesy of Hershey Kitchens, Hershey Foods Corporation, Hershey, PA. Used with permission.

PAGE 120/121 Land O'Lakes: Recipe and photo for Mom's Butter Cookies courtesy of Land O'Lakes, Inc. Used with permission.

PAGE 122 Hershey Foods: Recipe for Caroling Cookies courtesy of Hershey Kitchens, Hershey Foods Corporation, Hershey, PA. Used with permission.

PAGE 123 Land O'Lakes: Recipe for Russian Tea Cookies courtesy of Land O'Lakes, Inc. Used with permission.

PAGE 123 Pillsbury: Recipe for Moonbeam Cookies courtesy of the Pillsbury Bake-Off contest. Used with permission.

PAGE 124/125 Land O'Lakes: Recipe and photo for Browned-Butter Spritz courtesy of Land O'Lakes, Inc. Used with permission.

PAGE 126 Tone Brothers: Recipe for Candy Cane Cookies courtesy of Tone Brothers, Inc., producer of Tone's, Spice Islands, and Durkee products. Used with permission.

PAGE 127 Land O'Lakes: Recipe and photo for Fun Gingerbread Cutouts courtesy of Land O'Lakes, Inc. Used with permission.

PAGE 128 Domino: Recipe for Thumbprint Jewels courtesy of Domino Sugar. Used with permission.

PAGE 129 Land O'Lakes: Recipe and photo for Frosted Pepparkakor courtesy of Land O'Lakes, Inc. Used with permission.

PAGE 130 Domino: Recipe for Linzer Heart Cookies courtesy of Domino Sugar. Used with permission.

PAGE 131 Hershey Foods: Recipe for Sweetheart Kisses courtesy of Hershey Kitchens, Hershey Foods Corporation, Hershey, PA. Used with permission.

PAGE 132/133 Land O'Lakes: Recipe and photo for Easter Egg Cookies courtesy of Land O'Lakes, Inc. Used with permission.

PAGE 134/135 California Strawberry Commission: Recipe and photo for Fourth of July Cookie Pizza courtesy of ©California Strawberry Commission. All rights reserved. Used with permission.

PAGE 136 Hershey Foods: Recipe and photo for Halloween Cookies on a Stick courtesy of Hershey Kitchens, Hershey Foods Corporation, Hershey, PA. Used with permission.

PAGE 137 Domino: Recipe and photo for Jack-'o-Lantern Bars courtesy of Domino Sugar. Used with permission.

PAGE 138/139 Nutella: Recipe and photo for Spiced Sugar Cookies courtesy of Ferrero USA, manufacturer of Nutella hazelnut spread. Used with permission.

RODALE INC.
www.rodale.com

Birds Eye
www.birdseyefoods.com

California Strawberry Commission
www.calstrawberry.com

Cherry Marketing Institute
www.usacherries.com

Dole
www.dole.com

Domino
www.dominosugar.com

Duncan Hines
www.duncanhines.com

Hershey Foods
www.hersheykitchens.com

Kraft Foods
www.kraftfoods.com

Land O'Lakes
www.landolakes.com

McCormick
www.mccormick.com

McIlhenny Company
www.tabasco.com

National Association of Margarine Manufacturers
www.margarine.org

National Sunflower Association
www.sunflowernsa.com

Nutella
www.nutellausa.com

Ocean Spray Cranberries
www.oceanspray.com

Pillsbury
www.pillsbury.com

Quaker
www.quakeroatmeal.com

Skippy
www.peanutbutter.com

Sugar in the Raw
www.sugarintheraw.com

Sunkist
www.sunkist.com

Sun-Maid
www.sunmaid.com

Swans Down
www.swansdown.com

Tone Brothers
www.spiceadvice.com

Wisconsin Milk Marketing Board
www.wisdairy.com